# Endorsements

MARY SALAMON HAS WRITTEN the most practical guide for every citizen, let alone what every serious Christian, needs to understand how our Representational Democracy actually works. Every page clarifies in a direct way how each layer of our local, State and National government works and how individual citizens can understand this layered and complicated system. Many Christians think all levels of our government as confusing, corrupt, entangled in worldly values, dirty and beyond repair. They turn away from every mention of government while throwing their hands up in despair, feeling that average citizens could not possibly effect any change for the good. Christians know we are blessed with our form of government, but many are savoring the last days of the Republic and sadly believing there is no saving it now. In resignation, we are left to go on our lives just hoping nothing major will disrupt our freedoms and church community.

Mary shows us that there is another way to perceive our government! She shows us we can understand it and more importantly, steps laid out in this book will reduce our frustration and a sense of victimhood that characterize all too many Christians. Just as God is Lord over all of life, government is an area that important and Godly perspectives have much stability to add to it. Understanding there are steps that, beyond voting, every citizen can do to ensure our lives will be peaceful and actually benefit the weaker ones, protecting them and ordering our community lives. Her section of study questions would be excellent to discuss at the family dinner table, in a small group or a prayer group. Specific questions help us to think logically and expand our knowledge. As they say, knowledge is power. Many voices have decried this decade where so much has careened out of control in society but very few answers have been proposed. This book lays a groundwork for needed knowledge, understanding and presents the original purpose of godly standards in government that have now been eroding away. Without criticizing current positions, she lays out a place to begin and a track to run on. I see this book as an answer to "What can I do?" that so many are asking now. We Christian citizens can do this! Take one thing and start.

Thanks, Mary, for this helpful and motivating book!

**Virginia L. Chapman**
Church Awakening Prayer Coordinator

\*\*\*\*\*

MARY SALAMON'S NEW BOOK, *The Government and Its People—How The Church Can Participate in Government*, is a fresh and instructive primer in the basic role of the people of God as it pertains to society in general and the civil government in specific. The author skillfully weaves real life stories into this resourceful guide into the intimidating challenge of understanding the titles and duties of our civil leaders at every level. Mary also incorporates the mandate to pray for our leaders and does so in a very compelling manner I highly recommend this new and most timely teaching for citizens both young and old.

**Barbara Ingmire**
National Day of Prayer Task Force National Area Leader West
RPN WA State Leader

# The Government And Its People

## How The Church Can Participate In Government

2nd Edition

Mary Salamon

# Copyright

**The Government and Its People**

**How the Church Can Participate In Government–2nd Edition**

**by Mary Salamon**

Cover by Amani Hansen and David Munoz

Editing by Allison Hitz and Jim Bryson

Layout by Jim Bryson

# Dedication

THE MESSAGE OF THIS BOOK is dedicated to the Grace of God. I didn't pursue this message, the message pursued me. It eventually took me over and I was forced to write this book in order to get this message out of my heart and on paper. Government and Politics is not a popular subject, nor is it lighthearted to discuss and dissect. Even so, there are thousands of people that serve in government. This book is written to encourage and confirm that calling, but also to raise up thousands of Christians to answer the call to Civil Government. I want to thank my editors Allison Hitz and Jim Bryson. Alison began the journey with me and her work as an editor and proofreader are invaluable. Jim helped me finish the course with this project. Jim's experience as an editor brought me insight and helped me probe deeper into this subject as well as helping to add depth to my writing. The mountain of government needs to be climbed all the way to the top in order for the Gospel to continue to spread. This book is for all the climbers of that mountain.

# Contents

# Volume I

# Why The Church Should Participate In Government

# Introduction to Volume I

FOR MANY YEARS, I watched the news as a spectator. I cared little about state and world affairs. One reason was my upbringing. Our family was a sports family: football, baseball, softball, and basketball. Another reason was that my dad was a Teamsters Union employee and naturally gravitated to the Democratic Party. When asked what party affiliation we were, he'd boom out "Democrats!" adding that he hated Nixon. It was the same when Jehovah's Witnesses came to our door. "We're Catholics!" he'd say as he slammed the door. Ironically, we went to mass once a year. Yeah, you guessed it—Easter Sunday, adorned with all the fixings: a beautiful spring dress, an Easter bonnet, and white shiny shoes to complete the outfit.

Making matters worse, I continually heard this phrase in our home: "We never discuss politics and religion." As I grew into my adult years, I realized that it was a common saying with many people. And why not? It sounds so wise and philosophical. Yet today, I look at that phrase and think how ignorant and shallow it is. I know people who dodge these subjects to avoid combative discussions, but the downside is that at a certain level, there will always be parts of the relationship that will go unnoticed and unchallenged. As I look back on my upbringing, I realize that the reason my dad refused to discuss politics and religion is because we never participated in either culture.

In my early twenties, I became a Christian and joined a protestant church. I learned many wonderful things studying the Bible. Still, they believed that Christians were to separate themselves from the world and be fully engaged in church life instead. We were taught to engage people outside of the church only for the sake of evangelism. The core belief was that the more separated you were from the world, the more holy you were. Of course, we could engage in activities like sports or gardening, but even these activities could become idols if we spent more time weeding than reading our Bibles. Of course, politics and government were never discussed in this church. Instead, we heard:

"The church must obey God rather than men."

"We are not of this world. Our kingdom is a heavenly kingdom, not an earthly one."

And the final argument against engaging in politics, spoken with great conviction:

"Jesus was not political!"

Aside from my upbringing and current church environment, the fact was I never paid attention to politics and government due to my lack of understanding of how these worked. When I watched the news, I couldn't comprehend why particular issues and policies were geared a certain way. I felt the people running the government were exceptionally intelligent, as were the media people who reported it. Yet there were times when I would listen and say to myself, "Why can't I understand any of this?"

I remember watching Ronald Regan on television say these famous words: "Mr. Gorbachev, tear down this wall!" At the time, it meant nothing to me. I was more concerned with my family, my faith, and myself. I believed that the worldly, earthly government was dark and that nothing good came out of it. I believed the most important governments that existed were the church government and family. I was taught that everything will be better when Jesus returns and that we were to occupy until he comes, keeping busy saving souls and doing religious activities.

Then something profound happened to me. I became a homeschooling mom.

Well, there was a bit more to it. To instruct my children, I was forced to look at certain subjects more closely. Through homeschooling conventions, workshops, and seminars, I learned about the importance of solid teaching on civics, government, and history. In my quest to give my sons the best education I could provide, I began to absorb books on our founding fathers and other national heroes. As

I studied the curriculum to teach my children—easy-to-read books at first—I became obsessed with how amazing and blessed were our national leaders. I was stunned to learn that most were people of faith. I wept as I read about Abraham Lincoln, John Adams, and Daniel Webster. The crucial thing that resonated with me while studying was that God had placed his people in key, dominant, history-making roles. Those roles were outside the walls of the church and inside the very institutions I found to be oblique and religiously reprehensible.

Another profound influence—for me and millions of my generation—was the birth of talk radio.

Of course, conversation and family shows had been on the radio since the 1930s. However, this was the birth of political talk radio. The more I listened, the more I learned. I began to understand the issues, especially those important to my heart. I registered to vote and began keeping abreast of local, state, and national issues. I learned that politics is not hard to understand; a person just needs a good instructor. By listening to several radio hosts and the people calling in with their insights, opinions, and questions, I could comprehend complex political arguments that used to go right over my head.

Remarkably, changing my political views also changed my religious views. I realized that as a Christian—especially as a Christian—I had a responsibility to the country I called my home and in which I raised my children. According to Scripture, we are all given a *metron*—Greek for "a measure of rule." As citizens of the United States, our *metron* is the right to voice our opinion and give ourselves to different levels of government without fear of retribution.

Finally, the most profound revelation about government and my Christian faith was not that I had a rich heritage nationally, but that I had one scripturally. One day as I sat praying and meditating about the importance of Christians and government, the Lord showed me that almost every patriarch and prophet in Scripture either aided a government official or became one. It was like reading a Who's Who of the Bible. Government was established from the heart of God and given to his people. "For the LORD is our judge, the LORD is our lawgiver, the LORD is our king; it is he who will save us" (Isaiah 33:22). Any thinking person must conclude that even though Jesus is not political, he is the author of all righteous and just government, and his servants were governmental leaders. Consider the following from Dr. Robert Putnam of Harvard University:

> Over the last two decades the number of office seekers in any year at all levels in the American body politic—from school board to town council—shrank by perhaps 15 percent. As a result of this decline, Americans lost more than a quarter million candidates annually to choose among. It is impossible to know what price we paid collectively for the loss of those potential grassroots leaders—not only in terms of talent and creativity, but also in terms of competitive pressure on incumbent officeholders.[1]

Dr. Robert Putnam
Peter and Isabel Malkin
Professor of Public Policy
Harvard University

Imagine what our country would look like if Christians became the majority of the officeholders in the United States. Scripture tells us that Christians embody the wisdom of God—wisdom that is pure, peaceable, gentle, full of mercy with good fruits, impartial and sincere (James 3:17). All these attributes given to Christians through Christ's wisdom are the exact attributes ALL government leaders desperately need to rule and judge.

I can only imagine what price our country has paid because of the ignorance taught in many churches that Christians should avoid politics and government. It is impossible to know but staggering to contemplate.

In fulfilling my quest, this book is ammunition for Christians. It comes fully loaded with the why and the how of governmental engagement.

Why should Christians participate in government?

It is our God-given heritage.

How can Christians participate in government?

There are many creative and diverse ways to be involved in government from prayer to running for office.

This book examines the wonderful and awe-inspiring governmental roles that our forefathers were given and brings us to the present opportunities Christians can activate to make an impact on our country and the world.

Let's begin the journey and see where it takes us.

Mary Salamon

# 1

# <u>Worldviews</u>

SHOULD CHRISTIANS BE INVOLVED in politics and government?

The answer depends on your worldview. In simple terms, a worldview is how you see the world. James Sire's definition from The Universe Next Door is this:

> A worldview is a commitment, a fundamental orientation of the heart, that can be expressed as a story or in a set of presuppositions (assumptions which may be true, partially true or entirely false) which we hold (consciously or subconsciously, consistently or inconsistently) about the basic constitution of reality, and that provides the foundation on which we live and move and have our being.[2]

A worldview reflects the fundamental orientation of a person's heart. Christians, although united by a common God through Jesus Christ our Savior, possess a wide range of worldviews that affect how they see their role in government.

Consider the Scripture, "Do not love the world or anything in the world. If anyone loves the world, the love of the Father is not in them" (1 John 2:15). Depending on a person's heart orientation, they could interpret this verse as justification for hating the world—hate being the opposite of love. Another person with a different worldview, however, would consider John 3:16: "For God so loved the world that he gave his only begotten Son. That person would interpret 1 John 2:15 differently and so direct their heart to love the world in a way that seeks to improve it.

Interestingly, Christians with the worldview that loving the Father means hating the world are most likely to take the "watch and pray" approach to life, anticipating the imminent return of the Lord Jesus and therefore not being concerned with current events. Other Christians see involvement in politics and government as futile based on the belief that God is in control of everything. They conclude that Christians are not mandated by God to change a world that God is already minutely controlling. The question arises, however: Is God in control of every level and form of government? If so, why do we still have evil dictators controlling countries, robbing and slaughtering their people, and wreaking havoc throughout the world? The unavoidable conclusion of a worldview based on a controlling God is that somehow the evil prevalent in our society is the judgment of God and therefore is from God himself.

The far-ranging opinions of Christian involvement in government also include the worldview that government is inherently evil and should be judged by the Lord. Consequently, people ask, "Why get involved in an institution that has no redeeming qualities?" After all, Thomas Paine wrote, "Government, even in its best state, is but a necessary evil; in its worst state an intolerable one."[3]

Gregory Boyd, in *God of the Possible*, presents a cogent argument for the opposite viewpoint:

> When we rid ourselves of any lingering suspicion that evil somehow fits into the eternal purposes of God, we are more inclined to do something about it. Jesus spent his entire ministry revolting against the evil he confronted. He never suggested that any of the physical or spiritual afflictions he confronted somehow fit into his Father's plan. Rather, he confronted these things as coming from the Devil and carried out the Father's plan by healing people and delivering them. We who are Christ's disciples should follow our Master's lead.[4]

There could be several reasons why a person believes that government is evil and cannot be trusted. The first and strongest reason is that of injustice. When a person suffers unjustly from the government and no one comes to their aide, it causes deep mistrust and bitterness that can permeate many generations.

Others would counter, however, that while government has not always been fair and pure, we must recognize that this is due to the people in government positions and not government itself. When those holding authority rule unjustly through greed and lust for power, they cause great harm to others trying to live a peaceable life.

So, does God want Christians involved in politics and government, shaping the world according to his will? Or does he expect believers to shun the political system and, as some would believe, "Come out from among them and be separate" (2 Corinthians 6:17 NKJV).

We need to consider the nature of government before making up our minds on the issue. What do we mean, exactly, by "government"?

From a Biblical perspective, government exists to protect the people. This is why, when government fails in that purpose, it causes fear and anger in the hearts of people. Government is a creation from the heart of God, and as such is rooted in God's will. He established government at the beginning of creation when he created humankind to rule.

> *So God created man in his own image; in the image of God he created him; male and female he created them. Then God blessed them, and God said to them, "Be fruitful and multiply; fill the earth and subdue it; have dominion over the fish of the sea, over the birds of the air, and over every living thing that moves on the earth."*

> Genesis 1:27-28

Notice the phrase "have dominion over...." Obviously, dominion is equated with ruling and governing. And unless one assumes that man's rule included the abuse of everything under his authority—this was pre-fall, after all—it stands to reason that this God-given authoritarian structure was benevolent.

19

Interestingly, the first governing institution created by God was marriage. It even preceded the commissioning of Genesis 1:28. We know this by the account given in Genesis 1:27 above. Note that God's commission was to "them," as in "male and female he created them...." As in two, joined as one. In a word: *marriage.*

Elsewhere in Scripture, the Bible further delineates this governmental relationship, saying that the husband is the head of the wife.

> *For the husband is the head of the wife as Christ is the head of the church, his body, of which he is the Savior.*

Ephesians 5:32

Clearly, the husband has been given authority over the wife.

But why? The chief reason is to protect her, as understood by the phrase "as Christ is the head of the church." Jesus first and foremost protects his church out of love and from the strength that comes from ruling through God.

Using marital government as an example, when a husband fails to protect his wife, or in some cases controls and abuses her, he causes the institution of marriage to be distrusted. However, it is not that marital government is inherently evil, only that some people within marriage are evil. The institution itself is from God and is good.

Consider the role of government in property ownership. In most forms of government, there are laws and rules (procedures) in place to protect a person's right to own property. When someone tries to steal a person's property, the government's function is to declare such actions illegal and take appropriate steps to thwart the theft, thereby protecting the owner. Without such protections, ownership of anything would require constant warfare.

Of course, history tells us of unlawful confiscations of property by governments acting with impunity, of blatant racism and abuse of opposition. These glaring injustices are difficult to ignore and are often the reason that some embrace the worldview of "come out and be separate." By obeying a single Scripture—one that agrees with their worldview—they feel justified in ignoring the many other Scriptures that promote involvement in government, as well as denigrating opposing worldviews as "worldly."

> *However, the same abuses that cause some Christians to retreat drive other Christians to the worldview that not only should they be involved in government, but that they are vital to establishing God's principles and order at every level of government throughout the world. This perspective draws from Scriptures such as Jesus' parable of the ten talents. And he called his ten servants, and delivered them ten pounds, and said unto them, "Occupy till I come."*

Luke 19:13 KJV

While this parable has far-reaching implications, at the very least, it should counteract the worldview based solely on "come out and be separate." The definition of "occupy" used in Jesus' phrase, "occupy till I come," is this:

To take or fill up space; to be a resident or tenant; to hold a position or office; to take possession and control of a place, as by military invasion.[5]

It is difficult to derive justification from this Scripture for being passive or complacent. A person who is occupying is active, aggressive, and engaged with the people, places, and events that surround him or her.

In looking to the Bible as God's word—the expression of his authority and will—we observe that the writers of the New Testament often refer to the patriarchs' and the prophets' lives as examples of how we should conduct our lives. Peering into their experiences gives us insight to the way God leads a righteous person's life. We can learn from their mistakes and victories, their authority and power, and how they were appointed and positioned by God. Like gazing into a precious jewel with diverse facets, so it is when studying the people of the Bible. It holds layers of information, knowledge, wisdom, and understanding.

Many biblical leaders were involved in government. In fact, most of the patriarchs and prophets were either governmental leaders themselves, or they influenced top leaders and officials of their day. Consider how Jesus referred to Christians: "You are the salt of the earth. But if the salt loses its saltiness, how can it be made salty again? It is no longer good for anything, except to be thrown out and trampled underfoot. You are the light of the world. A town built on a hill cannot be hidden" (Matthew 5:13-14)

Light and salt are more than poetic symbols that we meditate on in our devotions. We must consider what actions coincide with being the light in the world and the salt of the earth. Light pierces, consumes, and fills the darkness. Salt was used as a preservative in the ancient world to ward off corruption. Jesus said that Christians are the salt of the earth. Throughout the Bible, salt was used for blessing to establish covenant and issuing judgment. If Christians are salt, we can inhibit the corruption of sin in this world with the living gospel.

Throughout our study, we will examine evidence supporting the belief that the Christian community should be actively involved in the political process and hold governmental offices at every level: neighborhood, city, county, state, and country. The Christian community is under a clarion call of God to fill the darkness with light and ward off corruption, not only the political world but the entire world and everything in it.

# 2

# <u>Where Government Begins</u>

I LIVE IN WASHINGTON STATE, a place where many pride themselves on being self-sufficient. We are the state of Lewis and Clark, those intrepid explorers who forged the way to the Pacific Northwest in a bold, rugged fashion. (Led by a very pregnant Native American squaw, incidentally.) Indeed, my nation, the United States, is known for the independent attitudes of its populace. We are citizens who believe in pulling ourselves up by our bootstraps. And yet, we are interconnected, dependent on each other in ways we do not always appreciate. Some of that connectivity is in the form of laws.

Whether we acknowledge them or not, rules and authority govern our everyday lives. Everywhere a person goes, authority rules over them. When we get into our cars, we better have up-to-date registration and insurance. As we drive away, must obey traffic laws. At work, our employer has authority over us. Rules and the authority they convey are everywhere—restaurants, grocery stores, schools, and even in our homes. We even need a building permit to add a room to our house— our very own house! Everything has an associated rule to follow.

Why?

For the sake of order, peace, and safety. So, where does authority come from? God, of course. It is not man-made; it was established from the beginning.

> *For by him all things were created, in heaven and on earth, visible and invisible, whether thrones or dominions or rulers or authorities—all things were created through him and for him.*

> Colossians 1:16 (ESV)

God created a world that runs on authority, and he instituted government to administer that authority, bringing peace and order to our lives.

Let's look closer at the tiers of authority that God created as identified in Colossians.

### Throne

- a ceremonial seat for rulers
- a chair of state having a footstool
- assigned to kings and queens, hence, royal power
- representing God's throne as the governor of the world
- representing Jesus Christ, the King of Kings, partner and assistant in the divine administration, hence all divine power belongs to Christ

### Dominion

- power, lordship

### Principalities:

- beginning, origin
- the person or thing that commences, the first person or thing in a series, the leader
- that by which anything begins to be, the active cause
- the extremity
- the first place of ruling angels and demons Power
- choice
- liberty to do as one pleases
- leave or permission
- physical or mental power
- the ability or strength one possesses or exercises.
- authority (influence) and of right (privilege)
- rule or government (the power of him whose will and commands must be submitted to by others and obeyed)
  a) universally: authority over all mankind.

b) specifically: the power of judicial decisions; the authority to manage domestic affairs

c) metonymically: a thing subject to authority or rule; jurisdiction; one who possesses authority; a ruler, a human magistrate.[6]

d) This covers every level of power, government, and authority in this world and beyond. Nothing and no one are outside God's authority, and Scripture says that all of this has all been given to Jesus.

*All authority [all power of rule] in heaven and on earth has been given to me.*

Matthew 28:18 (AMP)

Other scriptures continue this idea.

*Who is gone into heaven and is on the right hand of God; angels and authorities and powers being made subject unto him.*

1 Peter 3:22 (ESV)

*Far above all rule and authority and power and dominion, and above every name that is named, not only in this age but also in the one to come.*

Ephesians 1:21 (ESV)

*And ye are complete in him, which is the head of all principality and power.*

Colossians 2:10 (KJV)

*For to us a child is born, a son is given; and the government will be upon his shoulder, and his name will be called Wonderful Counselor, Mighty God, Everlasting Father, Prince of Peace. Of the increase of his government and of peace there will be no end, upon the throne of David, and over his kingdom to establish it and uphold it with justice and with righteousness from this time forth and forever more.*

Isaiah 9:6-7 (ESV)

Notice from Isaiah that God's government never ends. It continues to grow and expand. We will never escape it, nor should we.

So if God instituted governing and government, when did this government begin? For us, it began "In the beginning," when God created the heavens and the earth, as recorded in the book of Genesis. It expanded with the creation of man and his governance.

> *So, God created man in his own image, in the image of God he created him; male and female he created them. And God blessed them. And God said to them, "Be fruitful and multiply and fill the earth and subdue it, and have dominion over the fish of the sea and over the birds of the heavens and over every living thing that moves on the earth."*

Genesis 1:27-28(ESV)

According to Pat Robertson in his book, *The Secret Kingdom*:

Almighty God wants us to recapture the dominion man held in the beginning… The Genesis account uses two colorful words to describe this. One, *radah*, we translate "dominion." Man was to have dominion. The word means to "rule over" or "tread down," as with grapes. It comes from a Hebrew root meaning "spread out" or "prostrate." The picture we get from it is one of all the creation spread out before man, whose dominion would extend wherever his feet trod.

The other word, *kabash*, is translated "subdue." Man was told to subdue the earth. The root means "to trample underfoot," as one would do when washing dirty clothes. Therefore, in *kabash* we have in part the concept of separating good from evil by force. With the first word, *radah*, God gives man the authority to govern all that is willing to be governed. With the second, *kabash*, he grants man authority over the untamed and the rebellious. In both instances, God gave man a sweeping and total mandate of dominion over this planet and everything in it."[7]

In other words, God, who is supreme and has all authority, transferred that authority to humankind to rule and govern by the order he set in motion when he created the earth. While this may sound good at first, it presents an enormous challenge, one that humankind was never intended to face alone.

How do we carry out our God-given dominion and authority? Clearly, we do it through the institution of government. This is how we separate good and evil, the wise and the foolish, the just and the unjust. With the wisdom and mercy of God, we use laws, ordinances, and rules to live, govern, and reign in this world. This is what God had in mind when he commissioned Adam and Eve. Throughout the Bible, we see God delegating, transferring, and imparting his authority to people he has chosen to fulfill his plan for humankind. The forerunners, patriarchs, and prophets had specific roles to fill, and today, the Church has specific roles to fill. One role is to engage in modern government. In the proceeding chapters, we will examine how God appointed, prepared, and anointed his servants in governmental positions, establishing his will upon the earth and setting the example for us to follow.

# 3

# Process

AS WE STUDY THE LIVES OF THE SERVANTS OF GOD who were chosen to be in governmental roles, a dominant element stands out: process. This is the process that these chosen people endured to fulfill their role in God's plan. It was a process of qualification consisting of training, testing, and even sorting. Not everyone made it, but those who did served God mightily.

When we peer into the lives of forerunners like Joseph, Moses, and David, we discover that their processes were similar. Yes, they were naturally prepared to rule, but they were also tested and tried every way imaginable, their human spirits stretched, their hearts broken, and their wills brought into conformity with God's will. There was nothing easy about these processes, and we are naïve to expect anything different today.

**Process**

By definition, the word *process* means, "continuous series of actions meant to accomplish some result." The Lord God created process. As such, he is in the midst of the process. Why people endure tests and trials can only be understood when evaluating God's purposes for a process. In our study, we can view this in two ways:

1. the micro-process (detailed)
2. the macro-process (big picture)

The micro-process consists of the daily details of trials and testing, revealing how we respond to our unique circumstances. Through daily perseverance, we see the issues of our heart—our thoughts, motives, passions, and character traits comprising our personality. We evaluate our decision making; we face our mistakes and the needs they highlight. We discover how God uses the tiniest detail to enlarge our heart, to correct a deformity, and to perfect our soul.

Through the macro-process, we see how the Lord God takes things away while adding other things. The measuring scales are in his hands. While the micro-process is fascinating to study, it's the macro-process that reveals how the minute details fit together to form a larger picture. It's like a recipe. If want a perfect loaf of bread, the ingredients must be put together exactly as the recipe dictates. In these endeavors, we learn that there is a balance to perfection: not too much salt, just enough flour, warm water for yeast (not hot), and exact rising times. The final product—the bread—only comes out perfectly when we understand the importance of everything that goes into it. We can't take details for granted; a perfect loaf doesn't happen automatically. It takes time and effort. Nothing appears out of nowhere; even God's Spirit hovered over the faceless deep before God spoke creation into existence. And so it is for God's plan for his chosen servants. In his process, we learn to be patient and intentional.

Everything we know in our lives has an associated process. The macro-process reveals life as a whole—the big picture. To deny process in our lives is to deny our existence. Humankind is created for a God-given purpose and we are progressing to fill that purpose. Each generation is handed the torch from the previous generation to continue to walk out God's original mandate to be fruitful, multiply, and have dominion while living on this earth. Throughout history, we see how God is intricately moving humankind—how he intervenes, gets involved, blesses with innovation and invention, and increases knowledge and wisdom to human beings. We don't always see the hand of God at the micro-level, but it's hard to miss at the macro-level. The macro-level displays the positioning and timing of our God and reveals his grand purposes.

*To the intent that the living may know that the Most High*
*[God] rules the kingdom of mankind and gives it to*

*whomever he will and sets over it the humblest and lowliest of men.*

Daniel 4:17 (AMP)

The men and women of God recorded in the Bible were humble and lowly, though not at first, but they became that way by the shaping hand of God as he prepared them to rule and reign, thus establishing his will for humanity.

*His intent was that now, through the church, the manifold wisdom of God should be made known to the rulers and authorities in the heavenly realms…*

Ephesians 3:10

# 4

# <u>Joseph</u>

CONTRARY TO OUR WESTERN WORLDVIEW, the Bible identifies its leaders not as rugged individuals but as contributors to their family lineage, both natural and spiritual. As such, the God-given purpose of the patriarch Joseph's life did not begin with Joseph. It began with Jacob and Rachel, his parents. Jacob loved Rachel and wanted to marry her, but he had to marry her sister Leah first. So, he labored under their father for fourteen more years to finally have Rachel. After they married, several years passed before Rachel was able to conceive. Both she and Jacob went through dark trials and deep processes to have Joseph. Rachel was tried and tested time after time, watching her sister Leah give birth to one son after another for Jacob. Rachel lived in anguish and humiliation, and at one point she even wanted to die because of her infertility. When her son Joseph was finally born, she cried out, "God has taken away my reproach" (Genesis 30:23). Rachel was humbled from the beginning of her relationship with Jacob, not knowing she would birth a world leader leading to the Savior of the world. It was the process that qualified her.

Through this process, Jacob had twelve sons, including Joseph and Benjamin from Rachel. The Bible says that Jacob favored Joseph and kept him close. He even presented Joseph with a robe of many colors. Jacob loved his son Joseph more than all the others and likely doted on him. Because of Jacob's favoritism, however, sibling rivalry and jealousy arose between Joseph and his brothers.

> *But when his brothers saw that their father loved him more than all his brothers, they hated him and could not speak peacefully to him.*

> Genesis 37:4 (ESV)

This was probably made worse by a sense of entitlement on Joseph's part. (Read: spoiled.) Scripture doesn't specify this, but any parent will recognize the dynamic. For example, we read of Joseph running to his father and giving a bad report about his brothers' activities. Let's face it: the kid was a tattle-tale.

Unfortunately, Joseph then instills more hatred and jealousy by sharing a dream he had from God. In one dream, he declares:

> *he said to them, "Hear this dream that I have dreamed: Behold, we were binding sheaves in the field, and behold, my sheaf arose and stood upright. And behold, your sheaves gathered around it and bowed down to my sheaf." His brothers said to him, "Are you indeed to reign over us? Or are you indeed to rule over us?" So they hated him even more for his dreams and for his words.*

Genesis 37:6-8 (ESV)

Not content to leave well enough alone, Joseph shares another dream with his family, and the results are predictable.

> *Then he dreamed another dream and told it to his brothers and said, "Behold, I have dreamed another dream. Behold, the sun, the moon, and eleven stars were bowing down to me." But when he told it to his father and to his brothers, his father rebuked him and said to him, "What is this dream that you have dreamed? Shall I and your mother and your brothers indeed come to bow ourselves to the ground before you?" And his brothers were jealous of him, but his father kept the saying in mind.*

Genesis 37:9-11 (ESV)

You have to wonder if this kid was naïve or simply possessed of a death-wish. Either way, he sure didn't help his standing with his brothers. But remarkably, his actions ultimately placed him exactly where God wanted him.

Thus began the process of Joseph's journey in preparation for his life's call and destiny, even as he was dealt one injustice after another. He was sold into slavery to the Egyptians by his brothers. He became a slave in a man's household named Potiphar.

According to Dr. Charles Aling, Joseph would have been an Asiatic slave in the middle kingdom of Egypt. "One of the most common titles held by male Asiatic slaves was that of 'household servant.'" These slaves did a variety of tasks: serving, cooking, cleaning, and waiting on the master and his wife and children. Joseph was faithful and favored, so according to Scripture, Potiphar made him steward over his entire household.[8]

Charles Aling continues:

> Two of his subsidiary titles were "Scribe of Offerings" and "Chief of Agricultural slaves." The first proves that he was literate, and the second shows us his primary duty, the supervision of his master's agricultural estate.... This indicates two things about Joseph. First, he was literate. He would have to be to hold a stewardship. How and when he learned to read and write the complex Egyptian language is not known. Perhaps it was when he was a household servant of Potiphar. In any case, we may assume that Joseph was a quick and diligent student. Secondly, as a steward, Joseph would have been in charge of the agricultural holdings of his master, Potiphar. We should remember that ancient Egypt did not have a money economy as we know it today, and officials such as Potiphar would have been paid for their work by being allowed the use or ownership of farmlands. Potiphar would not have the time or perhaps even the skills to supervise the land and its cultivation himself; hence the necessity for a steward. We remember too that Joseph came from an agricultural family, and presumably already had extensive knowledge of farming techniques and farm animals.[9]

This was the beginning of an extensive preparation for Joseph to fill his future governmental role. (Spoiler alert: he becomes prime minister of Egypt, second only to Pharaoh.) To run Potiphar's household, Joseph had to learn to read and write the Egyptian language. It makes perfect sense, doesn't it? A person would have to know the language thoroughly to rule its nation. So, being taken into Egypt was not a punishment from God but instead a thorough preparation. It took time to prepare Joseph. His training included learning the language, being immersed in the culture, and understanding the economy. The Scriptures state that Potiphar's entire household was blessed because of Joseph.

Things went well for Joseph until another injustice happened to him. Joseph was wrongly accused of assault by Potiphar's wife. He soon found himself in prison. According to Charles Aling: As the Genesis account states, there was a "Warden" or "Overseer of the Prison," who was assisted by a large staff of clerks and scribes. Record keeping at such an institution was as important to the ancient Egyptians as it is in a modern prison. The actual title Overseer of the Prison is not commonly found in Egyptian inscriptions, but examples do exist from the Middle Kingdom, the time of Joseph.

One of the chief assistants to the Warden or Overseer was the "Scribe of the Prison." In Genesis 39:22 we are told that Joseph was promoted to high office in the prison. Since Joseph was literate, as we have seen from the fact that he served as steward in the household of Potiphar, it seems probable that he was promoted to Scribe of the Prison. As such, he would not only have been the right-hand man of the Warden, but he also would have been in charge of all the records of the institution.[10]

Yes, Joseph was favored once again. According to Genesis:

*The Lord was with Joseph and showed him steadfast love and gave him favor in the sight of the keeper of the prison. And the keeper of the prison put Joseph in charge of all the prisoners who were in the prison. Whatever was done there, he was the one who did it. The keeper of the prison paid no attention to anything that was in Joseph's charge, because the Lord was with him. And whatever he did, the Lord made it succeed.*

Genesis 39:21-23 (ESV)

Being the right-hand man of the warden meant that Joseph had full access to everyone entering and leaving the prison. Meanwhile, he was given the gift of dreams and their interpretation. Remarkably, when Pharaoh's butler and baker were sent to prison, they both had dreams. Joseph was able to interpret their dreams, and when the butler was released, Joseph asked the butler to remember him. According to Charles Aling, the butler was actually a cupbearer to Pharaoh.[11] he would have been in attendance serving Pharaoh all his beverages and so be in position to have Pharaoh's ear. He would have been the perfect man to plead Joseph's case, but the cupbearer forgot Joseph. Then came the day that the king had a dream that he could not interpret. The cupbearer finally told the king about Joseph's gift of interpreting dreams.

In Genesis 41, Pharaoh had two dreams. In one dream he was standing by the Nile,

*And behold, there came up out of the Nile seven cows attractive and plump, and they fed in the reed grass. And behold, seven other cows, ugly and thin, came up out of the Nile after them, and stood by the other cows on the bank of the Nile. And the ugly, thin cows ate up the seven attractive, plump cows.*

Genesis 41:2-4 (ESV)

Then Pharaoh had a second dream.

*And behold, seven ears of grain, plump and good, were growing on one stalk. And behold, after them sprouted seven*

*ears, thin and blighted by the east wind. And the thin ears swallowed up the seven plump, full ears.*

Genesis 41:5-7

Joseph finally appeared before Pharaoh, and he was able to interpret the dreams. He explained to Pharaoh about a future famine coming to Egypt. Joseph was then given instruction from God on how to prepare for the coming famine. He did such a good job protecting Egypt from starvation that God gave him favor with Pharaoh. Joseph was exalted to the second in command in all of Egypt—the most powerful country in the Middle East. Joseph ultimately became a father to Pharaoh, the lord of Pharaoh's entire household, and ruler of all Egypt under Pharaoh (ref. Genesis 45:8 ESV).

According to Charles Aling:

> The main job of the Chief Steward was the detailed supervision of the King's personal agricultural estates, the number of which would have been vast. This fits well with Joseph's advice regarding the coming years of plenty and the following years of famine. As Chief Steward, Joseph would be well placed to prepare for the coming famine during the years of more abundant production.[12]

It is interesting to observe that another specific responsibility of the Chief Steward was to take charge of the royal granaries, where the agricultural wealth of the nation was stored. As the person in charge of these great storehouses, Joseph was ideally placed for carrying out his suggestion to store food during the good years for the bad.[13]

Another title given to Joseph was "Ruler of all Egypt." This, according to Aling, could very well have been the position of Vizier of Egypt. This is strongly supported, and, if he was Vizier, Joseph's duties would have been similar to what we know as an ambassador and high official. Aling describes it as follows:

There are Egyptian inscriptions that describe the duties of the Vizier of Egypt…. Several texts exist which describe in great detail the duties and powers of the office of Vizier.

The Vizier was the chief record keeper of the government records, was the supervisor of the government in general, appointed lower officials of government to office, controlled access to the person of the Pharaoh, and generally supervised construction work and industry in Egypt's state-run economy. More pertinent to Joseph, the Vizier also was in charge of agricultural production, just what he needed to care for God's people in the time of famine.

Also, another power held by the Vizier has great interest in regard to the Joseph story. Only the Vizier welcomed foreign embassies coming into Egypt. So, when Joseph's brothers came to Egypt for food, they would normally meet with the Vizier. And, Joseph was the man they met.[14]

The account in the Bible demonstrates that God's calling and destiny for Joseph was to a position in one of the highest levels of Egyptian government—a position in a worldly government where the Lord gave him influence and power along with great authority to fulfill God's plan. Joseph's suffering, pruning, and testing were a preparation to fulfill a world-changing position in government.

What positions in our government today can we compare to those Joseph held so long ago? Joseph was a world leader, and he was used to save a nation. In our present day, the positions filled can be interpreted in several ways. There are problems in our environment that need answers. Who will be the ones to solve our nation's energy crisis? Who will be the ones to aid third-world nations in their fight against poverty and hunger? God is not just choosing one Joseph; Joseph is just an example for us to observe. God is looking for thousands of Josephs to save the world.

Are you one of them?

# 5

# Moses

OF ALL THE PATRIARCHS IN THE BIBLE, Moses stands as one of the greatest men who ever lived. If we believe the Bible is the inspired Word of God, then we must acknowledge that Moses was an amazing human being. No one else acted in the various offices and capacities as he did. He was a deliverer, a military hero, a prophet, a judge, and a lawgiver. He established a new religious system and integrated civil laws with religious observances. He wrote the first five books of the Bible, including the history and law of God's people. Finally, he brought the people out of their bondage in Egypt, led them through a dark wilderness season, and brought them to the brink of entering the Promised Land, passing the reins of leadership to his groomed successor Joshua.

Yet, it didn't start that way. In fact, it was many long years and much travail until Moses was prepared for the role God had for him. Let's look closer into Moses' preparation for his role in active government.

The process through which Moses became an outstanding leader was filled with suffering, trials, and intense training, coupled with faith, perseverance, signs, wonders, and miracles. Just as in the case of Joseph's parents who endured testing and trials, so it was with Moses's parents. Moses was born in Egypt at a time where the Bible says:

> There arose a new king over Egypt, who did not know Joseph.
> And he said to his people, "Behold, the people of Israel are
> too many and too mighty for us. Come, let us deal shrewdly
> with them, lest they multiply, and, if war breaks out, they join
> our enemies and fight against us and escape from the land."

*Therefore they set taskmasters over them to afflict them with heavy burdens…. But the more they were oppressed, the more they multiplied and the more they spread abroad. And the Egyptians were in dread of the people of Israel…. In all their work they ruthlessly made them work as slaves.*

Exodus 1:8-14 (ESV)

Despite Pharaoh's ardent desires, however, the people of Israel continued to multiply. Eventually, Pharaoh commanded every son born to the Hebrews to be thrown into the Nile, but the daughters were allowed to live. When Moses was born, his mother hid him for three months. The Bible states in Hebrews 11:23 (ESV) that he was hidden by his mother by faith because the child was beautiful and she was not afraid of the king's edict. Faith without works is dead, as we are told in James 2:14-22. In the midst of the turmoil, she made a desperate decision to release Moses into the Nile River in a woven basket.

What happened next was nothing short of miraculous.

*Now the daughter of Pharaoh came down to bathe at the river, while her young women walked beside the river. She saw the basket among the reeds and sent her servant woman, and she took it. When she opened it, she saw the child, and behold, the baby was crying. She took pity on him and said, "This is one of the Hebrews' children." Then his sister said to Pharaoh's daughter, "Shall I go and call you a nurse from the Hebrew women to nurse the child for you?" And Pharaoh's daughter said to her, "Go." So the girl went and called the child's mother. And Pharaoh's daughter said to her, "Take this child away and nurse him for me, and I will give you your wages." So the woman took the child and nursed him. When the child grew older, she brought him to Pharaoh's daughter, and he became her son. She named him Moses, "Because," she said, "I drew him out of the water."*

Exodus 2:5-10 (ESV)

For forty years, Moses lived as a son to Pharaoh's daughter and as a prince in the Egyptian court. According to Acts 7:22 (ESV), "Moses was educated in all the wisdom and culture of the Egyptians, and he was mighty (powerful) in his speech and deeds." We should note some important points from this Scripture alone.

Moses wasn't merely educated as the common people were; he was given the best education in the world at that time—an education was thorough and extensive, one befitting a future ruler of Egypt (as the plan most likely was).

According to Charles F. Aling in his book Egypt and Bible History, Moses's education came from the officials of the land. He received academic instruction as well as physical instruction. Moses was educated in hieroglyphic and hieratic scripts, spending endless hours copying and memorizing voluminous lists of words and names. He also studied foreign languages of the Near Eastern world. This probably included Akkadian (the language of Babylonia) and the Canaanite dialects. He also studied math, but the academic subject considered of primary importance was rhetoric. The Egyptians highly valued the ability to speak well in public, and accordingly, it received heavy attention during the years of formal education. Rhetoric in Egypt comprised not only public speaking but also proper style in writing.14

Being raised as a prince in Egypt meant that Moses was informed of the world in which he lived. He understood Egypt's culture, politics, and history. He was trained as a leader and military warrior. Ironically, while the Egyptians intended his education to be put to their use, it was really ordained by God in preparation for his role in delivering God's people from slavery and beginning a new nation, much to the detriment of Egypt. The new nation would be no ordinary nation, but one set apart to serve and honor the living God.

Of course, challenges abounded. The people of Israel would have to be taught to conduct their lives as free people. A new government would have to be established. God through Moses would have to establish new laws, rules, and ordinances. This was a monumental task, but not one given to Moses in a void of knowledge. Laws and ordinances that Moses could rely upon were established as far back as Abraham. With God's leading, Moses was able to improve upon them. When Moses wrote the biblical law, several cuneiform codes were being practiced throughout the Near East. According to Westbrook and Wells in their book Everyday Law in Biblical Israel, seven law codes have been recovered to date:

- Laws of Ur-Namma (LU), from the city of Ur in southern Mesopotamia, written in Sumerian and dating to around 2100 BC.
- The Laws of Lipit-Ishtar (LL), from the city of Isin in southern Mesopotamia, written in Sumerian and dating to around 1900 BC.
- The Laws of Eshnunna (LE), from a city of that name in northern Mesopotamia, written in Akkadian and dating to around 1800 BC.
- The Laws of Hammurabi (LH), from the city of Babylon, written in Arcadian and dating to around 1750 BC.
- The Middle Assyrian Laws (NBL), from the city of Sippar in central Mesopotamia, written in Akkadian and dating to the seventh century BC.
- The Neo-Babylonian Laws (NBL) from the city of Sippar in central Mesopotamia, written in Akkadian and dating to the seventh century BC.
- The Hittite Laws (HL), from Anatolia, written in cuneiform script in Hittite and dating between the sixteenth and twelfth centuries BC. [15]

All of these codes have similar laws and precepts. They extend through thousands of years and multiple cultures, yet the underlying principles of these laws remain the same. As stated in Everyday Law,

The biblical laws fit into this pattern. They are for the most part casuistic in form and contain many cases found in other law codes. The parallels between the biblical and cuneiform laws are the closest that any literary genre in the Bible has with an external source. They demonstrate that the clusters of everyday law are not a modern construction, but must already had had some independent existence in antiquity.[16]

What does this tell us about the laws of Moses? When Moses brought the people of Israel out of bondage, he issued laws and decrees that they were to live by. Some laws were already established and didn't need to be altered. Others were given by divine inspiration, mandated by God through Moses. For example, consider this law of Hammurabi from the city of Babylon:

If a man destroy the eye of another man, they shall destroy his eye. If one break a man's bone, they shall break his bone. If one destroy the eye of a freeman or break the bone of a freeman he shall pay one mana of silver. If one destroy the eye of a man's slave or break a bone of a man's slave he shall pay one-half his price. If a man knock out a tooth of a man of his own rank, they shall knock out his tooth. If one knock out a tooth of a freeman, he shall pay one-third mana of silver.[17]

This is the same law from Moses in Exodus 21:24(ESV) which states, "Eye for eye, tooth for tooth." Some say that Moses just copied the Hammurabi law. Others say that Moses wasn't even aware of the Hammurabi law. What is the truth?

With the education and training that Moses had as a prince of Egypt, he must have been fully aware of these other law codes, but to say he just copied them with no contemplation cannot be true either. In everything he did, he sought the wisdom of God. Most likely, he decided that there were some established laws that could be kept, and others that required change. Further, it's likely that the people he was leading were familiar with some of the laws. Would it not be prudent, then, to lead them with codes that they knew?

Of course, other laws of Moses represented a radical change. The first two commandments of the famous Ten Commandments display the fact that God was separating his people for Himself by demanding they worship him and him alone, having no other gods before Him. The people of Israel had just come out of severe bondage in Egypt. They had a difficult time even grasping that God alone needed to be worshiped. Indeed, if that weren't the case, they wouldn't have made a golden calf to worship while Moses was away to receive the very laws they were breaking. Obviously, they needed the additional laws.

As a lawgiver, Moses possessed godly wisdom to lead the people. As such, he used some existing laws—those based on universal principles—that the people of Israel already knew. He then skillfully integrated these with a new order of laws that God gave him. These laws established a holy and consecrated relationship with God.

The law code compiled by Moses included laws pertaining to people's daily lives. It covered damage to property, loss of property, injury, homicide, family law, hygiene, and sexual offenses. In forming this code, Moses faced the same challenges that lawgivers face today: Possessed of a deep sense of justice and understanding of their culture, how do they create laws in a way that benefits society as a whole while preserving individual liberty?

Today in the United States, thousands of laws exist. Most are good laws, though some lack common sense, and a few border on lunacy. Those who desire to be in government, particularly in the legislative branch, must apply prayer and sound principles to change unjust laws and create good laws—laws that allow us to live in peace and worship God in freedom.

# 6

# <u>Deborah</u>

AT THE TIME OF JUDGES, the nation of Israel was in flux. Moses had led them out of Egypt and through the desert, losing an entire generation of unbelieving ex-slaves in the process. Joshua had brought Israel into the Promised Land, but he had failed to complete his mission of total conquest, thus Israel was inhabiting a region influenced by Canaanite politics and religion. The 12 tribes of Israel were also split geographically by Canaanite cities that were not taken in the conquest, causing a deep divide in the nation. Because of this, the tribes struggled to unite as one nation in times of oppression and threats from foreign nations. In fact, some tribes were completely left to fend for themselves.

Moses and Joshua had been powerful, skilled leaders. Unfortunately, the tribes did not have a key leader at the time of Judges. Scripture states in Judges 3 that the Lord allowed foreign nations to test Israel so the Israelites would learn the art of war. Inevitably, the culture of these nations became integrated into everyday life for the people of Israel, so much so that they married the daughters of these foreign nations, gave their own daughters to marry other nations' sons, and ultimately served their gods.

This began a cycle where the people of Israel would abandon the Lord completely and commit apostasy with other nations. Then these nations that they turned to would rule and oppress them. Israel would then cry out to the Lord for deliverance. And the Lord would raise up deliverers to save them. At this time in history, these deliverers were called judges.

Interestingly, no judge presided in the office of judge except for one: Deborah.

Like Moses, Deborah filled more than just one role. She was a judge, military leader, and prophetess. Her name means "Bee," and Scripture says that she was the "wife of Lapidot." The Hebrew words are *eset lapidot*, which could also mean "woman of torches." Given Deborah's role in history, this author believes the term means "fiery woman." She was a charismatic, industrious woman, and whether she was married or not does not take away from her judicial and political role in Israel.

In the song of Deborah, a lengthy poem found in Judges 5, we can read of Israel's condition before Deborah rose in power.

> *In the days of Shamgar son of Anath,*
> *in the days of Jael, the highways were abandoned;*
> *travelers took to winding paths.*
> *Villagers in Israel would not fight;*
> *they held back until I, Deborah, arose,*
> *until I arose, a mother in Israel.*

Judges 5:6-7

According to Cundall and Morris, the word "highways" should be read as "caravans," meaning that commercial trading was impossible, and those who had to travel did so on the less-frequented routes to avoid being molested.[18]

"The villagers would not fight," implies that no one was actively involved in the protection and oversight of the people and their Deborah activities.

In the midst of this trouble, Deborah came on the scene as a leader and judge. She sat under the Palm of Deborah and made judicial decisions for the people, most likely the same kind of decisions that Moses made when he sat as judge, and later, as elders would do at the gates of Jerusalem. Initially, Moses sat with complete judicial authority, but then delegated his authority to able men from the elders and officials in the tribes (Deuteronomy 1:9-17 ESV).

At the time of Judges, the tribes of Israel were loosely bound together, and they did not have any specific courts or magistrates to settle their disputes. The Bible says that every person did what was right in his own eyes. How Deborah came to be judge is not mentioned. The Bible does not give much description or background of her life. It seems, however, that when disputes arose that the people could not settle between themselves, they came to her for judgment.

Deborah arose as "a mother in Israel." Another scripture coincides with the term "mother in Israel."

> *They used to say in former times, 'Let them but ask counsel at Abel,' and so they settled a matter. I'm one of those who are peaceable and faithful in Israel. You seek to destroy a city that is a mother in Israel. Why will you swallow up the heritage of the Lord?*

> 2 Samuel 20:18-19(ESV)

According to Susan Ackerman, Abel-Beth-Ma`acah was called "a mother in Israel" because people went there to ask counsel and settled their disputes.[19] What kind of decisions and disputes did Deborah settle? Likely, they would have been the casuistic laws that were followed universally in the whole region. As mentioned in an earlier chapter, casuistic laws affected people's everyday lives—damage to property, loss of property, injury, homicide, family law, and more. These contrasted with Apodictic laws which referred to divine commands of irrefutable truth.

Deborah was gifted with wisdom and authority to release justice as a mother to Israel. This mother symbol speaks of mercy and impartiality, as in a judge who would decide with great care and concern for both the plaintiff and defendant. In Isaiah 1:23, the Lord was displeased with Israel's existing rulers and judges because they loved bribes and did not defend the fatherless and widow.

> *Your rulers are rebels, partners with thieves;*
> *they all love bribes and chase after gifts.*
> *They do not defend the cause of the fatherless;*
> *the widow's case does not come before them.*

Yet in verse 26, the Lord promises to restore the judges once again.

*I will restore your leaders as in days of old,*
*your rulers as at the beginning.*
*Afterward you will be called*
*the City of Righteousness,*
*the Faithful City.*

Today, more than ever, we need judges who will decide according to basic humane principles that are fair to all; judges who will not favor people with money or power, or succumb to political pressure, but who will judge with courage and a good conscience so that humankind will not suffer when corruption is released. When corruption happens, it places a burden of despair on people, one that is incapable of being lifted without judges ruling according to basic, natural laws of justice, common sense, and fairness.

# 7

# <u>David and Solomon</u>

OF ALL THE CHARACTERS IN THE BIBLE who were called of God to participate in civil government, the rule of King David and then his son Solomon marks the end of one era and the beginning of another era—that of God's eternal government. God promised that he would establish a kingdom through David and that his throne would last forever.

> *Your house and your kingdom will endure forever before me; your throne will be established forever.*

> 2 Samuel 7:16

Of course, when Nathan the prophet gave this prophetic promise, who could have imagined that the Kingdom of God's government and rule would include people from every nation of the world? God chose David to begin his eternal kingdom, and he had a specific reason for doing so. In Acts, Paul explains that David was chosen because he was a man after God's heart, someone who would do God's will.

> *After removing Saul, he made David their king. God testified concerning him: "I have found David son of Jesse, a man after my own heart; he will do everything I want him to do."*

> Acts 13:22

The Scriptures say over and over that David's heart was perfect before God. One of the definitions for perfect is "whole." David served God with his whole heart; it was never divided, and he never served other religious gods or forms. He did make mistakes—some major mistakes—but he repented and God forgave him.

A few years ago, I was watching a Washington correspondent talk about his experiences interviewing several past presidents of the United States. One of his observations was that the men who became president didn't just arrive from out of nowhere. He said that there was a story, a background, and a process through which these men became president. Indeed, it was their stories that made their lives compelling.

David did not become king the day, or even the year, that God appointed him. It took several years of trials, testing, and suffering before he would be qualified to rule. He wasn't automatically handed the authority and the power of kingship. His character was formed and his patience tried. Under God's tutelage, David's process journey to rulership was deep and thorough.

Reading David's life story, it can seem that David's preparation was the exact opposite of what he was promised. David himself could not perceive the fullness to which he was called. He was chosen to be the king of Israel, and his son Solomon was eventually chosen to succeed him, but the Bible also reveals the promise of an eternal kingdom.

> *His seed shall endure forever, and his throne as the sun before Me [God], and it shall be established forever as the moon as a faithful witness in heaven.*

> Psalm 89:36-37 (ASV)

But what did that mean to David at the time? Did he see Israel established as a nation forever and ever on the earth? Did he know that God Himself would come in the flesh through his lineage and die for the sin of all humankind? Did he know that the Son of God would also be referred to as the Son of David? Did he know that more pages would be written about him on the earth than any other person who lived besides Christ Jesus?

David's extensive preparation was for both a temporal government and an eternal government. Our Lord Jesus came from the lineage of David, according to the promise that his seed would be established forever. David was chosen beforehand to walk in the work to which he was called. Those of us in Christ are also called to good works and to walk in them.

> *For we are his workmanship, created in Christ Jesus for good works, which God prepared beforehand, that we should walk in them.*

Ephesians 2:10 (ESV)

Faithfulness and perseverance are the keys. The reward is rulership. In the parable of the talents (Luke 19:11-27), we see that the servants that remained faithful to the Lord until he returned received cities to govern. God rewards with increased responsibility and authority to govern. It is an honor to rule governmentally. It is a reward.

Some Christians have more of a slave mentality than a ruler mentality. They think they are humble and pure by not being involved in politics and government, that even the Lord Himself would caution them to back away. These people are wrong. Our earthly life is preparation for eternity. We may not be called to the same vocations and occupations that we knew in this life, but we are called to be faithful and to rule over that which he has entrusted to us for eternity. Like David, we don't see all that God is preparing us for, but we know according to Scripture that we are destined to rule with Christ Jesus if we continue strong in the faith and remain obedient to his will for our lives.

Solomon was given the kingdom by his father. David prepared everything for his son to continue the reign, knowing it would be a daunting task. Solomon was wise enough to ask God for wisdom, knowing from his father's instruction that he couldn't reign without it.

> *Hear, my son, your father's instruction, and forsake not your mother's teaching,*
>
> *for they are a graceful garland for your head and pendants for your neck.*

Proverbs 1:8-9 (ESV)

Note the source of Solomon's teaching. He was admonished to receive both the instruction from his father and the teaching from his mother. Yes, Solomon was instructed from a young age in how to rule, yet when his time came, he cried out to the Lord for wisdom.

> *By me kings reign, and rulers decree what is just; by me princes rule, and nobles, all who govern justly.*

> Proverbs 8:15-16 (ESV)

This is the essence of administering justice.

What is justice? The basic definition is "the administering of deserved punishment or reward." The Oxford English Dictionary defines the just person as one who typically "does what is morally right" and is disposed to "giving everyone his or her due," offering the word "fair" as a synonym.[20] So justice is doing what is fair and right to everyone in society.

This means that everyone should receive the rewards that are due from their work and responsibilities. Therefore, injustice happens when men try to occupy positions in things they are not prepared for, appropriating rewards to which they are not entitled. Laws are created to give everyone their due.

This principle of giving everyone their due is administered through different types of justice. Differing worldviews and opinions exist regarding what is truly justice and how it should be applied. Further, this subject has been at the core of ethics and morality debates for centuries. Justice has several layers; therefore, it makes sense that people's sense of justice differs depending on the individual case and circumstances.

Justice must be based on what is fair, what is right, and what is moral. And even though the core remains the same, there are different applications of justice, primarily: distribution, retribution, and restoration.

Distribution can also be called social justice because it deals with economics and the goods and services people receive. Many believe that goods should be distributed simply by need. Others believe that other criteria should govern, such as earning as the right to possession.

Retribution is corrective justice. This involves punishing a person for crimes against humanity. This justice involves making clear decisions and ensuring that the punishment meets the crime. For instance, we wouldn't stone someone to death for stealing from a cash register.

Restitution is also called restorative justice, and it presents itself in various ways. Fundamentally, it means that the person who has been injured or robbed should be compensated for their loss. Determining what is fair compensation is an aspect of this justice. Justice is not just about obeying the laws, however. Historically, the poor are afflicted and taken advantage of by the rich. We see this in literature, including the writings of Charles Dickens, which often illustrate what Scripture is trying to convey. The poor are shown no mercy because of the greed of their overseers. Hence the scriptural admonishment.

*Rob not the poor, because he is poor, or crush the afflicted at the gate*

Proverbs 22:22

*For I know your manifold transgressions and your mighty sins: they afflict the just, they take a bribe, and they turn aside the poor in the gate from their right.*

Amos 5:12 (KJV)

According to the Bible, the poor have rights, but they do not have a right to be wicked, lazy, or covetous. According to the parable of the talents (Luke 19:12-26), the man who only had one pound and did nothing with it, had that pound taken away and given to the man with ten pounds. Covetousness is not against the law of civil court, but it is addressed by the tenth commandment according to the Law of Moses.

*You shall not covet your neighbor's house. You shall not covet your neighbor's wife, or his male or female servant, his ox or donkey, or anything that belongs to your neighbor.*

Exodus 20:17

This admonishment against covetousness is further echoed throughout the New Testament, giving credence to the fact that we do have natural rights in society.

So, what does it mean to covet? According to Dictionary.com, "covet" means, "to desire wrongfully, inordinately, or without due regard for the rights of others."[21] According to the Bible, a person is not allowed to covet that which they have no right to possess. The positive benefit of this is that people have a right to their own things and relationships without fear of someone else misappropriating them. This principle is deeply embedded in our consciousness and our hearts, as borne out by the proclamation of the prophet Amos.

*But let justice roll down like waters, and righteousness like an ever-flowing stream.*

Amos 5:24 (ESV)

Justice flows from the heart of God.

Solomon asked for wisdom to rule, and it was given to him. In Proverbs, he detailed how people should live out their lives in order, peace, and harmony. Solomon was not given a set of laws to rule by, but a heart of wisdom and understanding for how people should live and conduct their affairs.

Whether it is a city mayor, a state governor, or the President of the United States, if the ruler is God-fearing, they can ask for wisdom and receive discernment on how to apply justice. Consider the promise of God embedded in James.

*If any of you lacks wisdom, let him ask God, who gives generously to all without reproach, and it will be given him.*

James 1:5 (ESV)

The most efficient, just, and fair leaders will be those leading and discerning with godly wisdom—the same wisdom given to King Solomon.

# 8

# <u>Elijah</u>

ELIJAH WAS A FIERY PROPHET sent by God to confront a feckless King Ahab. Historically, the facts are that King Ahab was a powerful ruler in the Near East. He was the son of Omri, the king of Israel who established Samaria as his capital. Omri was a major figure in international affairs, a strong military commander and developer of enormous building projects. In the book, *The Bible Unearthed*, by Finkelstein and Silberman, the authors write:

> Samaria was the most grandiose architectural manifestation of the rule of Omri and Ahab. It was a royal acropolis of five acres that can be compared in audacity and extravagance (though perhaps not in size) only to the work that Herod the Great carried out almost a millennium later on the Temple Mount in Jerusalem.[22]

Ahab continued to expand the dynasty his father began. He operated a huge army, conducted large building projects and built cities. Then he married Jezebel, the daughter of the Phoenician king Ethbaal. According to Finkelstein and Silberman, marrying Jezebel could have been looked upon historically as a brilliant stroke of international diplomacy.[23] It was not a brilliant action, however, according to the writers of the Hebrew Bible.

> *And Ahab the son of Omri did evil in the sight of the Lord, more than all who were before him. And as if it had been a light thing for him to walk in the sins of Jeroboam the son of Nebat, he took for his wife Jezebel the daughter of Ethbaal king of the Sidonians, and went and served Baal and worshiped him. He erected an altar for Baal in the house of*

*Baal, which he built in Samaria. And Ahab made an Asherah.*
*Ahab did more to provoke the Lord, the God of Israel, to*
*anger than all the kings of Israel who were before him.*

1 Kings 16:30-33 (ESV)

It's never a good thing to have written that a king did more to provoke the Lord to anger more than all the other kings before him. All the grandeur of the Israelite kingdom meant nothing compared to the national sins being committed in the capital of Samaria. The Lord did not take lightly this insurrection to his commands and precepts. Because of Ahab's pride in his prominence and achievements, he wasn't going to be corrected by just a prophetic word from a prophet. He would have to be confronted with acts of judgment. To that end, the Lord called the prophet Elijah to defy Ahab and Jezebel. This was no small task.

Elijah was called to confront one of the most powerful kings of Israel. In so doing, he was facing head-on the wickedness of an entire nation. Elijah was a prophet of fire whose name means "Yahweh is God." He was anointed with signs, wonders, and miracles to confront the deep inroads that Baal worship had made in the hearts of God's people. The people of God were being deceived by Baal's prophets. Baal was worshiped as the king of the gods as well as the god of storms and fertility. Because these were vital elements to the everyday lives of Israel, Baal worship played an active role in the people's existence.

Elijah was appointed by God to expose the lies perpetrated by the prophets of Baal who said that Yahweh was just another God. Every act of Elijah was ordained to challenge people's faith in Baal. He confronted them, stating that they were vacillating between two beliefs—Baal and the Lord God. Elijah was ordained to show that Baal was nothing compared to God.

Elijah, through the power of God, confronted Baal worship in the areas of its supposed authority—the weather and growing seasons. Elijah declared a drought on the land. There was no rain for three years and the famine in Samaria was severe. God took away the rain to display his authority over the elements. This left Ahab in a desperate situation. Then God raised the stakes.

> *After many days the word of the Lord came to Elijah, in the third year, saying, "Go, show yourself to Ahab, and I will send rain upon the earth."*

1 Kings 18:1

At first glance, this might appear to be good news to Ahab—the drought is over. But remember, the battle was not over rain in Israel, but to settle the question of who would reign in Israel. Elijah opposed Ahab directly with the authority of the Lord God, and when he declared the drought over, he did so with the same authority.

Elijah was displaying governmental authority. He was a governmental prophet called to rebuke the highest form of government. This authority came with power and went much further than challenging the influence of a local demonic religion. God, through Elijah, was extending the fight to the hearts and minds of the people. When Ahab saw Elijah, Ahab said to him, "Is it you, you troubler of Israel?" And he answered, "I have not troubled Israel, but you have, and your father's house, because you have abandoned the commandments of the Lord and followed the Baals. Now therefore send and gather all Israel to me at Mount Carmel, and the 450 prophets of Baal and the 400 prophets of Asherah, who eat at Jezebel's table."

> *So Ahab sent to all the people of Israel and gathered the prophets together at Mount Carmel. And Elijah came near to all the people and said, "How long will you go limping between two different opinions? If the Lord is God, follow him; but if Baal, then follow him." And the people did not answer him a word.*

1 King 18:17-21 (ESV)

Elijah challenged the prophets of Baal with power and fire in one of the greatest spectacles recorded in Scripture. Both sides prepared a sacrifice upon an altar, and the god who answered by consuming the sacrifice with fire would be God in all the land.

The prophets of Baal went first, crying out all day, cutting themselves with swords and pleading to their god, but there was no answer from Baal. Then toward evening, it was Elijah's turn. But before he asked God to consume his sacrifice, he ordered his altar to be drenched with water, not once but three times. Then he prayed.

> *And at the time of the offering of the oblation, Elijah the prophet came near and said, "O Lord, God of Abraham, Isaac, and Israel, let it be known this day that you are God in Israel, and that I am your servant, and that I have done all these things at your word. Answer me, O Lord, answer me, that this people may know that you, O Lord, are God, and that you have turned their hearts back."*

Then God answered Elijah's prayer.

> *Then the fire of the Lord fell and consumed the burnt offering and the wood and the stones and the dust, and licked up the water that was in the trench.*

1 King 18:36-38 (ESV)

There were no more questions in the hearts of the people. The Lord was God, and now, it was judgement time.

> *And when all the people saw it, they fell on their faces and said, "The Lord, he is God; the Lord, he is God." And Elijah said to them, "Seize the prophets of Baal; let not one of them escape." And they seized them. And Elijah brought them down to the brook Kishon and slaughtered them there.*

1 King 18:39-40 (ESV)

That day at Mount Carmel was a day of judgement, cleansing, restoration, and appearing. One lone prophet of God stood against 450 prophets of Baal and won. This was no easy task. The prophets of Baal served at Jezebel's table. They were high and powerful in the government of Ahab. They were not only spiritual prophets but political prophets as well, active in the community and governmental affairs. They led the people of Israel astray and kept them in deep darkness, causing them to turn away from the one true God.

Yet, even though this display of God's power was a decisive victory that turned the Lord's people back to Him, it did not fully root out the corruption in the government. Elijah thought there had been a thorough cleansing of the Baal culture, but to his astonishment, it didn't touch the heart of Jezebel. The defeat of Baal only enraged Jezebel more, causing her to threaten Elijah's life. He ran into a cave where he began to question God.

Elijah, despite his great power from God, became so discouraged that he thought he was the only faithful believer left in Israel. However, God corrected him saying:

> *Yet I will leave seven thousand in Israel, all the knees that have not bowed to Baal, and every mouth that has not kissed him.*

1 Kings 19:18 (ESV)

God showed Elijah that feeling isolated and being isolated are two different things. Eventually, because of Elijah's faithfulness to God, Jezebel was dealt a final blow, bringing to an end the heart of Baal worship in Israel.

This victory could not have come had Elijah not exercised his God-given authority to challenge the government. We have similar authority today. Christians living in the United States also have authority to challenge their government. Our authority comes from God as we worship and obey the Lord, and that same authority flows down to the foundation of our government.

Governments are instituted among men, deriving their just powers from the consent of the governed.

**The Declaration of Independence**

Our authority begins with the Constitution of the United States and includes the first 10 amendments to the Constitution, commonly called The Bill of Rights.

The Bill of Rights was established to safeguard an individual's rights by placing limits on the power of the government. The very first line in the first amendment is this:

> Congress shall make no law respecting an establishment of religion, or prohibiting the free exercise thereof.

Christians living in the United States have the freedom to worship God openly. It is the law of the land. And because of that, we can stand up for our beliefs and defend them when called upon to do so.

Ecclesiastes 3:7 states that there is a time to keep silent and a time to speak. Sometimes our governmental leaders need to be openly rebuked when they begin to sway public opinion against our religious freedom and even persecute Christians for their deeply held beliefs. The law is on our side, and that is the grace of God.

In this world, because of the media, Internet, and diverse political persuasions, it's easy to believe that just a few people still follow after God's heart. But in reality, there are many, and we are growing in number all over the world. The Lord will continue to raise up prophets of fire and rain to declare to the whole world and its governments that "the Lord, he is God!"

# 9

# Government and the Prophets

WHEN STUDYING THE SCRIPTURES on God and Government, some will argue that the Old Testament has no bearing on what God is doing today through his Church. Yet the scriptures below testify that the things written before Christ are for our learning.

*For whatsoever things were written aforetime were written for our learning, that we through patience and comfort of the scriptures might have hope.*

Romans 15:4 (ESV)

*Now these things happened to them as an example, but they were written down for our instruction, on whom the end of the ages has come.*

I Corinthians 10:11 (ESV)

The Lord God established his people and formed a nation. Within that nation, there was the priesthood and the civil authority. He would be the King, and he chose Moses to be a judge and prophet, and Aaron to lead the people in the temple. As time passed, Israel desired a king like their neighboring nations. This desire hurt and probably devastated our Father. Our Father is our creator and knows what is best for his family, but he gave them what they wanted, and from that new government, kings were anointed and appointed to rule over the nation.

The Lord didn't stop with the kings. He still had the priesthood to worship him and to train his people to worship and serve his holy covenant. His covenant didn't when he allowed his people to have kings, and he also added another layer of accountability to the kings. This accountability came in the persons of prophets. Almost every prophet in the Bible was assigned to a king, kings, or a nation. The prophets were seers, visionaries, miracle workers, and fiery preachers who were absorbed in the culture of their day. Most of all, however, the prophets were governmental. As such, the prophets were always aware of the political landscape during their time. They helped lead the nation and were God's mouthpiece.

Following is a synopsis of the prophets and their kings:

- Isaiah called Judah and its kings to repent and return to God or face judgment. Isaiah served the southern kingdom of Judah under the reigns of four kings of Judah. The kings that reigned during Isaiah's time were Uzziah, Jotham, Ahaz and Hezekiah. Isaiah prophesied to King Hezekiah and said that the Assyrians and their King Sennacherib would fall before Judah. The angel of the Lord struck 185,000 down in the camp of the Assyrians. Isaiah moved in the miraculous. God moved the sun back ten steps as a sign to King Hezekiah that God would add 15 years to Hezekiah's life. Isaiah was stripped naked and barefoot in obedience to God as a "sign and wonder" against the Egyptians for three years. He was highly esteemed by the people and the leaders of his day. He was faithful to Israel and her Kings.

- Jeremiah was a prophet who warned Judah of judgment if they did not repent. He is considered the weeping prophet in the Bible because he cried out to Judah for forty years to repent and turn from their wickedness. Jeremiah served God under the reigns of five kings; Josiah, Jehoahaz, Jehoiakim, Jehoiachin, and Zedekiah.

- Ezekiel prophesied to Judah during their time in exile in Babylon.

- Daniel was also a prophet to Judah during their captivity in Babylon. Daniel served four kings, Nebuchadnezzar, Belshazzar, Darius the Mede, and Cyrus the Persia.
- Hosea called Israel back to God. Israel had begun worshiping other gods and was unfaithful to the one true God. Hosea is known for being a personal object lesson for Israel as God called him to marry an unfaithful woman to show Israel what they were doing to him. During his ministry, wicked kings ruled Israel; Jeroboam II, Zechariah, Shallum, Menahem, Pekahiah, Pekah, and Hoshea.
- Joel was a prophet to Judah, warning them that they must repent or face judgment.
- Amos was a shepherd who God called to tell Israel to stop mistreating the poor among them. He served under Jeroboam II.
- Obadiah is just one chapter long and is a prophecy against the nation of Edom because they were hostile to Jacob's descendants. Remember, Edom was the name given to Esau, Jacob's twin brother.
- Jonah was called to prophesy against the city of Nineveh.
- Micah warned Judah to turn back to God or face judgment. The kings were Jotham, Ahaz, and Hezekiah.
- Nahum also prophesied against Nineveh, but this time after the Assyrians (Nineveh was in the Assyrian empire) had captured the Northern Kingdom of Israel. The kings were Manasseh, Amon, and Josiah.
- Habakkuk is a book of questions that he had for God. He is pondering the why of evil in the world.
- Zephaniah called Judah back to God and promised that the faithful could look forward to when God judged the wicked. The King was Josiah.
- Haggai prophesied to Judah as they returned from exile in Babylon and began rebuilding Jerusalem.

- <u>Zechariah</u> prophesied to those returning to Judah from exile in Babylon.
- <u>Malachi</u> prophesied to Judah after they returned from exile in Babylon and called for them to repent.
- <u>Elijah</u> was the prophet to Ahab, Ahaziah, and Joram.
- <u>Elisha</u> was the prophet to Joram, Jehu, Jehoahaz, and Jehoash.

There were also other prophets. Samuel anointed two kings, David and Saul, and he judged another king named Agag. In 1 Samuel, the Lord commanded King Saul to exterminate all the Amalekites and all they owned, including livestock (1 Samuel 15:1-3). King Saul did the exact opposite. He kept the livestock and chose to keep King Agag alive. Samuel confronted Saul with his disobedience and killed King Agag before the Lord. Killing Agag was a military act that King Saul should have performed. Samuel then prophesied to Saul that the kingdom would be torn from him, even as Saul tore at Samuel's robe. Samuel then found David and anointed him as King.

According to Gotquestions.org and the Bible:

> Nathan and Gad were prophets called to David's side. Gad was a prophet and seer who counseled David. When David fled from Saul, Gad advised him to return to the land of Judah (1 Samuel 22:5). After David sinned by taking a census, Gad rebuked him and offered a choice of punishments, and David chose a plague (2 Samuel 24:11-14). Gad advised King David to build an altar on the threshing floor of Araunah the Jebusite on the day the plague ended (2 Samuel 24:18-19). Gad also aided in the arrangement of Levitical music (2 Chronicles 29:25). In 1 Chronicles 29:29, Gad is said to have written a part of the history of the life of King David.[24]

> Nathan was a prophet in the Bible who lived during the reign of King David in Israel. God spoke to David through Nathan on several occasions. Nathan was a member of David's royal court and one of his closest advisers. Nathan apparently also

knew Bathsheba well enough to speak to her about Adonijah's attempt to usurp David's throne from her son, Solomon (1 Kings 1:11) and to enlist her help in bringing the matter to the King. There are three or four stories in the Bible featuring Nathan that occurred during some of the darkest and most emotional times in David's life.

The first mention of Nathan establishes his relationship with David as a trusted adviser. David decides to build God a house, because the King is living in a beautiful cedar palace and thinks it wrong that the Ark of the Covenant should be housed in a lowly tent (the tabernacle). David tells Nathan about his plans to build a house for God, and Nathan says he should go ahead and do it because the Lord is with him (2 Samuel 7:2-3). Then God visits Nathan in a vision and tells him to return to David and inform him that God doesn't need the King to build him a house; rather, God would establish David's dynasty, through his son, forever. His son Solomon would be the one to build God's house (2 Samuel 7:4-17). Nathan relays this important message to the King, and David utters a grateful and beautiful prayer to God for his grace (2 Samuel 7:18-29).

The next time Nathan is mentioned, it is after David had committed adultery with Bathsheba and brought about her husband's death to hide her pregnancy (2 Samuel 12:1). At that point, David had made Bathsheba his wife and had seemingly gotten away with his sin, but the Lord knew about it and told Nathan to rebuke David. Nathan went to David and wisely told the King a fable about a rich man and a poor man: the rich man was visited by a traveler, so he took the poor man's only possession, a little ewe lamb that he loved as a pet, to feed his guest—rather than taking a lamb from his own extensive flocks. David was enraged at the story and declared that the rich man had no pity and deserved to die. Nathan then points to David and says, "You are the man!" (2 Samuel 12:7). Nathan reveals that David's sin was like that of the rich man, because David took away Uriah's wife. Nathan then prophesies to David, in God's own words: "I anointed you King over Israel, and I delivered you out of the hand of Saul. And I gave you your master's house and your master's wives into your arms and gave you the house of Israel and of Judah. And if this were too little, I would add to you as much more. Why have you despised the word of the LORD, to do what is evil in his sight? you have struck down Uriah the Hittite with the sword and have taken his wife to be your wife and have killed him with the sword of the Ammonites. Now therefore the sword shall never depart from your house, because you have despised me and have taken the wife of Uriah the Hittite to be your wife" (2 Samuel 12:7-10). David confesses to Nathan that he has sinned against the Lord, and Nathan comforts him, saying that the Lord has forgiven his sin and that David's life will not be required of him. Nonetheless, David's child by Bathsheba was to die. David, under inspiration of the Holy Spirit, pens Psalm 51 after this encounter with Nathan the prophet.

After the death of David's child, his wife Bathsheba became pregnant again, this time with a son whom they named Solomon. The Lord sent Nathan to David again, this time to say that the Lord loved his son Solomon, and they called Solomon "Jedidiah," a name that means "beloved of the Lord" (2 Samuel 12:24-25). Solomon later built God's house, the temple, and became an ancestor of the Lord Jesus Christ.

First Chronicles 3:5 reveals the fact that King David and Queen Bathsheba named one of their sons born to them in Jerusalem "Nathan." No doubt, the child's name is a reflection of the royal couple's appreciation for the prophet Nathan's faithfulness, friendship, and tough love through the years."[25]

These prophets stood in the highest courts of government and were used as instruments of God's hand in leading King David, as well as instructing, correcting, and judging King David and the nation he ruled over. David's son, Solomon, became the wisest ruler and built the temple of God exactly as his Father David instructed. But then Solomon allowed his many wives to turn his heart from the Lord, and a prophet named Ahijah the Shilonite prophesied that the kingdom would be torn from Solomon. (ref. 1Kings 11:29)

The prophets in scripture were national prophets with governmental mantels. God placed his authority on them to govern along with the kings. Are there national prophets today? Yes! These prophets may not have the title of a prophet, but they speak and minister to leaders worldwide.

# 10

# Daniel

THE PROPHET DANIEL DECLARED to King Nebuchadnezzar of Babylon that God rules the kingdom of men and gives it to whomever he wills, even the lowest of men.

*The Most High is sovereign over all kingdoms on earth and gives them to anyone he wishes and sets over them the lowliest of people.*

Daniel 4:17 (ESV)

At this time in Israel's history, the Jews were captives of Babylon. Because of the sins and apostasy of God's people, they had been overthrown and enslaved by the Babylonians. They no longer had the privilege of being a nation. Instead, they had to learn to live again in a foreign land with a different religion and culture. Chaldean culture was widespread among the Babylonians. It was from this culture that the Babylonians perfected the art of magic. This included the activities of magicians, sorcerers, and enchanters, and the use of omens, incantations, astrology, and other occult practices to tell the future and search for hidden mysteries. King Nebuchadnezzar ordered his court official—the master of the eunuchs—to bring the most promising youths from the exiled Jews to be trained in his court. These youths were to be of royal seed and nobility. The Bible states that they were without blemish, well-favored, skillful in all wisdom, and endued with knowledge and understanding of science. The master of the eunuchs was directed to teach the youths the language and culture of the Chaldeans. Four of the chosen were Daniel, Hananiah, Mishael, and Azariah.

Joyce G. Baldwin writes that the study of Babylonian literature was a completely alien world to these young men of Judah.

According to the Sumerians and Babylonians, two classes of persons inhabited the universe: the human race and the gods. Pre-eminence belonged to the gods, though they were not all equal. At the lower end of the divine scale came a host of minor deities and demons, while a trinity of great gods— Anu, Enlil, and Ea—stood at their head. A modern scholar will observe that many of these gods are personifications of parts or aspects of nature. The sun and moon gods are obvious examples.[26]

Because of the king's order, Daniel and his companions were brought into the highest level of Babylonian government. As part of their training, their names were changed from Hebrew names to Babylonian names. Further, they were expected to serve and obey the king and his laws, learn the culture of Babylon, and live within the prevailing culture.

In conforming to the king's wishes while staying true to God, Daniel serves as an example of how Christians should live in this present world. Most countries today are led by secular governments. These governments have no allegiance to Jesus Christ or his work. Instead, they look to themselves for the solutions to difficult problems in leading their nations. Still, if they are good governments, they will follow godly principles even if they do not acknowledge the source of these principles. Daniel and his companions were endowed with godly wisdom, and it raised their stature in the Babylonian kingdom. Daniel was able to be useful to a secular government while still maintaining his firm faith in God. Notice that during his training in Babylonian culture, Daniel and his companions refused to eat at the king's table. This was no small thing. It could have cost the life of the official who was in charge of their well-being.

Scripture states that eating at the king's table would have defiled Daniel. This defilement was not necessarily dietary because, as Baldwin points out:

All food in Babylon and Assyria was ritually unclean, and from that there was not escape. Daniel 11:26 (ESV) provides more light as to why he refused to eat at the king's table. "Even those who eat his food shall break him." By eastern standards, to share a meal was to commit oneself to friendship; it was of covenant significance.[27]

In the East, partaking at one's table is deeply relational. Still, Daniel had not arrived at the king's court by his own volition. He was taken as a servant. Therefore, he was not there to commit his heart to the king in friendship through sharing a meal; he was there to serve and represent God to a godless nation. The Lord guided Daniel and protected him in these daily decisions. Daniel learned to walk out his life before the Lord while being established in a secular government.

Because of the obedience of Daniel and his companions:

*The king had appointed for them to be brought before him, and the king conversed with them, and among them none were found like Daniel and his companions. The king found them ten times wiser than all the magicians and enchanters who wherein his whole realm.*

Daniel 1:19-20 (AMP)

Daniel and his friends stood out and apart from the rest of the king's court. They were given wisdom and spiritual gifts to serve the king with depth and accuracy. They excelled in their discernment and interpretation of dreams and visions because the Lord positioned them and equipped them to perform their duties to the king.

Daniel served as an adviser to four kings: Nebuchadnezzar, Belshazzar, Darius, and Cyrus. The Lord displayed his knowledge, power, and protection while administering his judgment and decrees differently to each king.

Here are some ways that God showed himself as the ultimate ruler of all mankind:

1. Nebuchadnezzar had a dream that troubled him. He called upon his cabinet of magicians, enchanters, soothsayers, sorcerers, and diviners to tell the king what he had dreamed and what it meant. They could not tell the king and stated that no man on earth could show the king his dream. Nebuchadnezzar then decreed that the wise men of Babylon were to be killed. This included Daniel and his companions. Daniel asked the king for some time and then he and his companions sought the Lord in prayer, and the dream with the interpretation was given to Daniel. Daniel cried out of his heart,

> *"[The Lord] reveals deep and hidden things;*
> *he knows what is in the darkness,*
> *and the light dwells with him.*
> *To you, O God of my fathers,*
> *I give thanks and praise,*
> *for you have given me wisdom and might,*
> *and have now made known to me what we asked of you,*
> *for you have made known to us the king's matter."*
>
> Daniel 2:22-23 (ESV)

2. Nebuchadnezzar made an image of gold. Then he sent for every government official and cabinet member to be at the dedication of his golden image. He asked for the satraps, deputies, governors, judges, chief stargazers, treasurers, counselors, sheriffs, lawyers, and every other chief official. It was one important national event! he commanded that when the people heard the sound of music, they were to fall down and worship the golden image. Whoever did not bow down and worship would be cast into a fiery furnace that very hour (Daniel 3). Of course, Daniel's three friends refused to bow to the golden image. This was reported to the king, and it enraged him. He confronted Shadrach, Meshach, and Abednego, and threatened to cast them into the fiery furnace, asking them what

god could deliver them out of his hands. They responded by saying that God will deliver them, but even if he didn't, they would not serve the king's gods or worship his golden image. In the end, these three men of God were delivered out of the fiery furnace without even a whiff of smoke on them, causing a heathen king to bless and praise the living God.

3. Belshazzar became king after Nebuchadnezzar. By that time, Daniel had been made chief of the magicians, enchanters, soothsayers, and astrologers because he was known to have an excellent spirit, knowledge, and understanding to interpret dreams, clarify riddles, and solve knotty problems. When he was called upon by the king to read the famous "writing on the wall," Daniel declared to the king that the end of his kingdom was at hand. The king was slain that very night.

4. Darius became king and promoted Daniel to a high governmental office, being chosen to share rule over the entire kingdom with two other officials. But Daniel became so distinguished above the other officials that the king planned to set him over the whole kingdom. That stirred up a jealous spirit among the other two officials, and they conspired against Daniel, coming against his personal prayer life and intercession. King Darius had issued an edict requiring that all people pray to him, and to him alone, for thirty days. Daniel refused and was thrown into the lions' den for praying to his god. And yet, God delivered Daniel, causing Darius to make a decree stating that the Lord is the living God, enduring forever, that his kingdom shall never be destroyed, and his dominion shall never end. The end of Daniel 6 states that Daniel prospered during the reigns of Darius and Cyrus the Persian.

Daniel and his companions worked and lived among those whose beliefs, morals, and values were not only different but were often blasphemous to a holy God. And yet, this was by God's design. The Lord could have supplied a quiet community for his servants to live in—a hiding place far from the center of current political events and the upheavals of changing times. Instead, the Lord God placed his chosen servants in the middle of the culture where he protected, promoted, and prospered them. It was there that they thrived, demonstrating that it's not the external environment that makes the difference in a believer's life, but whether they are in the will of God.

Daniel was in the highest levels of government and thrived in his relationship with God. Indeed, not only did he survive, but his spiritual life flourished. His kingdom prophecies are still being studied today.

Daniel and his friends serve as examples of how we can serve God in a secular government. They were given solutions and shown "the writing on the wall" while refusing to bow or worship any other gods. They drew their lines and the Lord kept them safe and prosperous, proving over and over again that he was the only true living God, now and forever.

# 11

# Esther

THE BOOK OF ESTHER IS A FASCINATING STORY that stands out differently than the books of Daniel and Nehemiah with regards to the attitude, convictions, and worldview of the Jewish people. Esther is unique among the books of the Bible because God is not mentioned and there is no reference to his laws. In the story, Esther and her uncle Mordecai were living in Sousa fifty years after Cyrus the king decreed that the Jewish people could go back to Jerusalem to rebuild the temple. King Xerxes, also known as Ahasuerus, took the throne in 486 BC. He was the second Persian king following Darius the Mede.

For years, the famous declaration from Esther, "And who knows whether you have not come to the kingdom for such a time as this?" (Esther 4:14), has been quoted and glamorized in sermons and prophetic utterances. Those words mean, of course, that Esther was chosen by God for a special time and place in history. Yet, a closer look at the circumstances that caused Esther to become queen is baffling and questionable.

Culturally and politically, Esther and Mordecai were rooted in Susa. If that wasn't the case, they would have easily relocated to Jerusalem at some point in their personal timeline. Apparently, they were comfortable and established in the Persian environment. Further, Mordecai was not an invisible citizen in Susa; he was likely from nobility and well known in both the Jewish community and the Persian government. How do we know this? Because Mordecai sat at the gate of the palace (Esther 2:21 ESV).

According to jewishBible.org:

The name Mordecai is mentioned 58 times in the Book of Esther. Five times he is referred to as Mordecai Hayehudi, usually translated, "Mordecai the Jew." Perhaps a better translation might be "the Jewish Judge," for all five times refer to Mordecai in an official capacity... The phrase "sitting at the gate" is a common Biblical way of referring to a member of the court of justice... Bible critics agree with classical Jewish commentators that the phrase "gates" usually means courts.

The Talmud reports the tradition that Mordecai was the head of the Jewish court. Since it was usually Persian policy, except during times of religious persecution, to give considerable independence to ethnic minorities, it would have been probable for King Ahasuerus or his predecessor to have appointed or affirmed the appointment of a Jewish judge, possibly giving him an official title or at least a name as Belshazzar gave Daniel.[28]

Mordecai had so much influence in the Persian government that he was able to get information to King Xerxes about a secret plot to assassinate him, warning the king in time and saving his life. Later, as an established government official, Mordecai not only persuaded Esther to prepare herself with hundreds of other virgins to come before the king but was also able to secretly get her through the process without any of the Persian officials' knowledge of her Jewish origins.

At first glance, this seems like a shrewd move, which in fact it is, but take note that Mordecai insisted on deception to get Esther through the courts of the king. He lied and Esther lied. Not only is lying involved but also the complete dismissal of the law of Moses and God's covenant. The law explicitly states that God's people were not to engage in marriage outside the Jewish faith. In the instance of Mordecai and Esther, Mordecai brought his own relative in to engage in a sexual union with a pagan king before there was any hint of marriage.

Esther submitted to Mordecai as her father and elder, but she also showed no resistance in any capacity in preparing herself to sleep with a pagan king. In fact, the goal was to so please him in bed that she might become queen instead of Vashti. To put this plainly, this would be like a Christian parent instructing their virgin daughter or son to deny they are a Christian and have sexual intercourse with a mayor, governor, congressperson, or president in order to gain access to these high-level positions. This is unthinkable for a Christian. It seems that Mordecai was maneuvering and manipulating his niece, advising her in such a way that would benefit his goals and aspirations.

And yet this is precisely how God saved the Jewish people.

The story of Esther displays more concern about politics and nationalism than about the observance of God's laws. This brings to mind Paul's observation that "now we see through a glass, darkly" (1 Corinthians 13:12 KJV). God and his Word give entrance to light and truth. So before we judge Mordecai and Esther, recall that others in the Bible compromised their godly principles as well.

- Abraham gave his wife Sarah over to a pagan king, using her beauty and sexuality in exchange for favor and protection.
- Jacob deceived his brother into giving up his birthright.
- Moses murdered an Egyptian.
- Joseph was a tattletale.
- David was an adulterer and murdered an innocent man to cover it up.

But God....

- But God saved Sarah, telling the pagan king that if he touched her, he'd be a dead man.
- But God used Jacob and his two wives to birth the 12 tribes of Israel.
- But God used Moses's fear of conviction to drive him deep into the desert to develop him into a man of God.
- But God raised up Joseph as a deliverer not only of his own people but of Egypt as well.

- But God established David and Solomon in the lineage of Jesus.

Although human beings are far from perfect, God always sees beyond what the human eye can discern. God perceives in our hearts depths and underpinnings that are impossible for us to detect. A deeper look at the story of Esther reveals truth and light, bringing the Lord God and his covenant promise to the forefront of history. As stated earlier, we know from Daniel 4 that the Lord God rules the kingdom of men and gives it to whom he wills.

In the story of Esther, two prominent positions are taken away and reassigned by God's sovereign hand. The Bible states that the king of Persia loved Esther more than all the virgins presented to him, and so he made her queen. Acting on the counsel of Mordecai, she gained one of the highest positions possible—the wife of a king. Mordecai had already attained a position, but God had more ordained for him. Through human agents, God continued to display his faithfulness and justice. He is not a man that he should lie (Numbers 23:19). What he says he will do, he does.

Mordecai had a bitter enemy; his name was Haman. These two men despised each other. Interestingly, a universal bond connected them, one originating hundreds of years before they are even born. In Esther 2:5, read that Mordecai was the son of Jair, son of Shimei, son of Kish, a Benjamite. Saul, Israel's first king, was also the son of a man named Kish, a Benjamite. In Esther 3, Haman was identified as "Haman the Agagite." Agag was the king of Amalek. The Amalekites were bitter enemies of Israel during Saul's reign. Haman was a descendant of King Agag. The crux of this is that Mordecai and Haman were the representatives of two nations—one nation blessed by God through covenant with Him, and the other an enemy of God.

Remember, nothing happens out of nothing. King Saul disobeyed God's instructions to kill the captured King Agag. Instead, he allowed him to live and even seemed to befriend him. For this disobedience (and others) Saul lost his throne.

Generations later, God still had issues to resolve because of Saul's disobedience. As descendants of Saul, Mordecai, and Esther were positioned to deal with the wicked root of the Amalekites as represented by Haman. God's sovereign will was being manifested through their conflict.

Esther found so much favor with the king of Persia that, through a series of remarkable events, the king decreed that all of Haman's household be killed. He then gave Esther authority to have thousands more killed by declaring that the Jews had the right to defend themselves from those sent out to slaughter them. She was also given the authority to institute the Jewish feast of Purim, a feast that is still celebrated today. Haman had sought to destroy the Jews and cast out Mordecai, but instead, the reverse happened. Scripture says that Mordecai grew greater and stronger in the king's palace.

In our present time, it is disturbing to contemplate the fact that nations are still at war and killing each other. As a Christian leader in government, it would be a hard decision to send troops off to war. It's an extremely difficult choice for any leader to command the death of thousands, yet in the Old Testament, it happened over and over. Esther was not afraid to issue the decree. Indeed, she did what she had to do to preserve her heritage.

The debate on war and peace will continue. In the meantime, remember that Esther was elevated to one of the highest positions in government not based on her education or skills, as she had no experience in governmental affairs. It wasn't about what she knew, but whom she knew. Her promotion was based solely on personal relationships. Her honor and respect gave her great authority and much reward. As the wife of a king, she honored her husband and saved a nation.

While observing governmental leaders today, everyone knows how powerful the influence of a close relative can be, especially in making difficult decisions. Governmental leaders need mentors, good friends, and family to support them, pray for them, and give them counsel when asked. You may be one of those who support an official. If so, the counsel you give could very well change a nation.

# 12

# Nehemiah

IN BIBLE DAYS, THE LIFE OF THE KING was in constant danger from those who would use his death to advance their own position. That is why the royal cupbearer was such an important position. It was his job to protect the king from poison drink. He did this by drinking the wine before the king drank. If the cupbearer died, well, at least the king was saved. Given his proximity to the king, the cupbearer usually developed intimate access to the king and the influence that went with it (assuming the cupbearer lived long enough). Cupbearers were well known in the palace and at court, and in many instances became the king's confidants.

Nehemiah was the cupbearer of King Artaxerxes I, the Persian king whose domain included Jerusalem. When observing Nehemiah's life, we see specific characteristics and attributes that gave him great favor with King Artaxerxes. The Bible does not state how he rose to that prestigious position, but he was positioned to fill an assignment that would bring him to Jerusalem and fulfill God's promise to rebuild the city walls. The Persian empire ruled Jerusalem, and King Artaxerxes had stopped the rebuilding of the city and its walls because of lies warning him of rebellion if the rebuilding was allowed to continue (Ezra 4:7-23 ESV). In Nehemiah 1, Nehemiah was given a report on the condition of Jerusalem. It was not good news. The walls of Jerusalem were broken down and its gates were burned. In response, he humbled himself with prayer and fasting before the Lord. He wept, repented, and prayed for several months until God gave him strength, vision, and hope for the future of the project. With all that God did for him, Nehemiah plotted out a strategy to accomplish a nearly impossible task. It would require great favor and assistance from Artaxerxes—things that Nehemiah was positioned to acquire.

One of the reasons Nehemiah found favor with the Persian king was his sincere loyalty to the well-being of the king. This influence started when the king asked Nehemiah why his face was so sad. In response, Nehemiah first honored Artaxerxes's authority. Nehemiah had proved his faithfulness to the king by keeping him alive, so when the king heard why Nehemiah was sad and asked him what he wanted, Nehemiah was not afraid to tell the king everything.

> *In the month of Nisan, in the twentieth year of King Artaxerxes, when wine was before him, I took up the wine and gave it to the king. Now I had not been sad in his presence. And the king said to me, "Why is your face sad, seeing you are not sick? This is nothing but sadness of the heart." Then I was very much afraid. I said to the king, "Let the king live forever! Why should not my face be sad, when the city, the place of my fathers' graves, lies in ruins, and its gates have been destroyed by fire?"*
>
> *Then the king said to me, "What are you requesting?" So I prayed to the God of heaven.*
>
> Nehemiah 2:1-4 (ESV)

Nehemiah was specific about how he wanted to rebuild the walls of Jerusalem; he held nothing back. He laid out a plan before the king for what he would need, how long it would take, and how to arrive safely at his destination. He explained all of this in detail to King Artaxerxes. In turn, the king gave him everything he requested.

> *And the king granted me what I asked, for the good hand of my God was upon me.*
>
> Nehemiah 2:8 (ESV)

Nehemiah received a depth of favor that caused Artaxerxes to reverse his own policy and finance the whole building project. How did this happen? Several keys are here to meditate on why Nehemiah received everything he asked.

- Nehemiah was positioned in a high level of government. This position was established by God. As stated earlier, cupbearer positions were one of the closest to the king. Cupbearers became companions and trusted confidants to the king and queen and many other officials in the court. Nehemiah had proved his loyalty and faithfulness.
- Nehemiah was full of the wisdom of God. He depended on God to answer his prayers while recognizing fully where and how those prayers could be answered.
- Nehemiah wasn't afraid to ask the king for assistance with everything he needed.
- Nehemiah was a visionary and a strategist. He researched and acquired all the information he needed to get the task done.
- Nehemiah had courage. He wasn't afraid of executing the plan, or of asking a king to reverse his edict and allow the rebuilding of the walls. Equipped with authority and supplies, Nehemiah went to Jerusalem to rebuild the walls—completing a task that he was burdened from God to do. He left the Persian palace as a faithful follower, but to rebuild the walls, he had to become a strong, faithful, leader.

According to Nehemiah 3, Nehemiah broke down the project into different sections and manageable sizes. For labor, he was able to mobilize the whole community to get to work. Not just one or two groups were involved. His leadership skills brought together all types of workers—priests, city officials, temple servants, goldsmiths, and merchants. Even men who lived outside of Jerusalem came and worked—men from Jericho, Tekoa, Gibeon, Mizpah, Zanoah, Beth Hakkerem, Beth Zur, and Keilah.

His authority, leadership, and organizational skills brought the rebuilding of the walls to a completion in 52 days! Although it was not without opposition. The same hostility and resistance that halted the vision years before came back to challenge Nehemiah.

The first opposing force came from those who would be the most threatened by the new governor and the rebuilding of Jerusalem. Sanballat and Tobiah were governors in the region; Sanballat was the governor of Samaria, and Tobiah was the governor of Amman. Both men ridicule and threaten the work.

The first thing Nehemiah did in response to this opposition was to pray. He didn't try to retaliate with physical force; instead, he asked God to vindicate him. When the fight did become real, Nehemiah used the same organizational skills that got the king to approve the project in the first place. He formed a defense mechanism that ensured the building project would be completed while also defending God's people from attack. He used both the spiritual and natural to combat the opposition. He inspired his people to be courageous, but he also gave placed natural weapons in their hands to defend themselves and their families. In so doing, he took his enemies' threats seriously, but never succumbed to fear, relying instead on God's divine protection. The most important thing Nehemiah did, however, was to KEEP WORKING. He was not persuaded in any way to delay the work; it progressed through the most intense opposition.

In addition to the external opposition, resistance also came from within.

> *Now the men and their wives raised a great outcry against their fellow Jews. Some were saying, "We and our sons and daughters are numerous; in order for us to eat and stay alive, we must get grain."*

> *Others were saying, "We are mortgaging our fields, our vineyards, and our homes to get grain during the famine."*

*Still others were saying, "We have had to borrow money to pay the king's tax on our fields and vineyards. Although we are of the same flesh and blood as our fellow Jews and though our children are as good as theirs, yet we have to subject our sons and daughters to slavery. Some of our daughters have already been enslaved, but we are powerless, because our fields and our vineyards belong to others."*

Nehemiah 5:1-5

In response to these charges, Nehemiah became angry and confronted the nobles and officials, demanding that they give back to the people their fields and vineyards, and insisting that they stop charging the people interest. He also refused to take what other governors in the past demanded, saying, "But the earlier governors—those preceding me—placed a heavy burden on the people and took forty shekels of silver from them in addition to food and wine" (Nehemiah 5:15 NIV).

Clearly what was happening with some of the treatment of his Jewish brothers was not noble or generous. In fact, it was just the opposite. The poor were being exploited by their own. It was illegal and unjust. Nehemiah makes no excuses for the rich but defends the poor in the gates the way a servant of God should do.

*But the noble make noble plans, and by noble deeds they stand.*

Isaiah 32:8

In the Amplified Bible, we read:

*The noble, openhearted, and liberal man devises noble things; and he stands for what is noble, openhearted, and generous.*

The poor need a defender, not an excuser. Nowhere in these Scriptures does it say that the poor were not working or willing to work.

Everyone was asked to help rebuild; everyone had a stake in the success of the rebuilding. As a man of God, Nehemiah knew that the wealthy Jews were disobeying the law of God. Leviticus reads:

> *If your brother becomes poor and cannot maintain himself with you, you shall support him as though he were a stranger and a sojourner, and he shall live with you. Take no interest from him or profit, but fear your God, that your brother may live beside you. You shall not lend him your money at interest, nor give him your food for profit. "If your brother becomes poor beside you and sells himself to you, you shall not make him serve as a slave."*

Leviticus 25:35-37, 39 (ESV)

Nehemiah had to correct the situation. He had to set things in order so that everyone would be in agreement. This was an internal situation, but how could the plan and vision proceed and prosper without addressing the fatal flaws within his own people? The plan would have failed eventually due to the injustice to the poor and the violations of God's word.

Nehemiah led by example as the governor of Judah. He showed a generous spirit when he refused to take benefits available to him. This enabled the people of Judah to trust his leadership and believe his word. He established a unity among the people so that they appeared and stood before him with one heart. As governor, he instituted national reforms with Ezra the priest. The reading of God's word, prayer, and the service of the temple were all brought back at a national level.

By definition, a *miracle* is "an effector extraordinary event in the physical world that surpasses all known human or natural powers and is ascribed to a supernatural cause." Nehemiah's accomplishments were miraculous acts. According to James Boice, this is the order of Nehemiah's acts that were accomplished in less than one year as governor of Judah:

1. Nehemiah secured Artaxerxes's permission to rebuild the walls of the desolated city. He received permission to go rebuild the walls as well as to reverse a previously established policy regarding Jerusalem.
2. Nehemiah developed a plan for constructing the walls.
3. Nehemiah inspired a defeated and dispirited people. This was important because the people had tried to build before and had failed. It was nearly one hundred years of failure. Nehemiah had to lift them into faith.
4. Nehemiah overcame opposition from outside enemies and from inside his own people.
5. Nehemiah completed the reconstruction of the wall.
6. Nehemiah encouraged and assisted in a national revival with Ezra the priest.
7. Nehemiah reorganized and repopulated the city.[29]

These astounding accomplishments were done through faith, persistence, and courage in God. The fact remains, however, that they were also accomplished through the support of the Persian government. We see that the Church can accomplish important things through government. Large building projects can only be completed with the favor and assistance of city and state officials. Nehemiah is an example of how a person can be positioned to equip and lead people in the practical application of ministry.

# 13

# Was Jesus a Political Activist?

AS A MOTHER AND NOW A GRANDMOTHER, I celebrate Christmas by sharing food, gifts, and singing with family and friends. It's a special time of the year because we choose this time to celebrate the birth of our Lord and Savior, Jesus Christ. Over the years, I have heard many sermons about Jesus' humble beginnings. He was born in a manager, raised in a modest home, and took up a lowly occupation. He suffered the most humiliating death that a human being can endure. We were taught to be meek and humble as Jesus was, and that this was the only true gospel. In many churches, loving and serving people are at the heart of most teachings in the pulpit. I have been told countless times that Jesus, our God, was humble and never political or governmental.

The fact is, Jesus is not a Democrat or Republican. He's not a citizen of the United States, and he doesn't want his church involved in political and governmental activities. In fact, in writing my book, I pondered the name: *God, I Know You're Not a Republican, But I Pray You're Not a Democrat Either.* As a Christian, I know God is not a Republican; indeed, he's not affiliated with any political party. Yet the question I pose is: was Jesus political?

From his birth, Jesus came to shake government and governmental structures.

*After Jesus was born in Bethlehem of Judea in the days of Herod, the King, behold, wise men from the east came to Jerusalem, saying, "Where is he who has been born King of the Jews? We saw his star when it rose and have come to worship Him."*

Matthew 2:1-2 (ESV)

Jesus is called a king at birth. His birth threatened the rule of King Herod. Kings rule and govern. The scripture doesn't say "Let us worship a priest." It reads "Let us worship a king."

When Jesus became a man and the Spirit of the Lord came upon Him, he entered his ministry. He openly confronted the Pharisees and Sadducees for their corruption and greed, especially for how they twisted the scriptures. The Pharisees and Sadducees were not just religious leaders. They were also the political leaders of Israel. Israel was called Judah at the time, renamed Judea by the Romans. Judea was an occupied territory of Rome. However, the Romans did not run everything in Judea; not even close. As long as the Jews paid their taxes and didn't revolt, Rome had little interest in their internal affairs. The Jews had their own police (temple guard) and public jail (Acts 5:18).

According to Julian Spriggs:

> It was the normal Roman practice to leave most of the running of the government to local leaders. In Judea, this was the Sanhedrin, dominated by the Sadducees and ruled by the High Priest. In return for their support for the Roman rule, the Sadducees kept their wealth and privileged position secure. The Sanhedrin were the overseers of the chief legislative, judicial, and religious functions. Members of the Sanhedrin were the equivalent of the congress and senators that represent us today. [30]

According to Bill O'Reilly, in *Killing Jesus*,

> The Sanhedrin was a court comprised of seventy-one judges with absolute authority to enforce Jewish religious law, except for in the case of a death sentence. In that case, they must get the approval of the Roman governor. The Sanhedrin

is the ultimate Jewish religious court, a body of men even more powerful than the tetrarch Antipas. And within this chamber, Caiaphas, the High Priest born into a centuries-long lineage of wealthy Temple priests, holds the ultimate authority.[31]

Why is this information important?

It's essential to understand the governmental rule during Jesus's time, and if Jesus himself engaged or confronted governmental rulers. Was Jesus a political activist? At birth, he was called a king, and Kings are rulers, and he is the King of kings and the Ruler of rulers. He didn't raise an army or establish a new government before his death, but was he a political activist?

There was only one group of people that Jesus confronted with his anger and rebuke.

> *But woe to you, scribes and Pharisees, hypocrites! For you shut the kingdom of heaven in people's faces. For you neither enter yourselves nor allow those, who would enter to go in. Woe to you, scribes and Pharisees, hypocrites! For you travel across sea and land to make a single proselyte, and when he becomes a proselyte, you make him twice as much a child of hell as yourselves.*

> Matthew 23:13-15 (ESV)

> *Woe to you, scribes and Pharisees, hypocrites! For you are like whitewashed tombs, which outwardly appear beautiful, but within are full of dead people's bones and all uncleanness. So, you also outwardly appear righteous to others, but within you are full of hypocrisy and lawlessness.*

> Matthew 23:27-28 (ESV)

> *Woe to you, scribes and Pharisees, hypocrites! For you build the tombs of the prophets and decorate the monuments of the righteous, saying, 'If we had lived in the days of our fathers,*

*we would not have taken part with them in shedding the blood of the prophets.' Thus, you witness against yourselves that you are sons of those who murdered the prophets. Fill up, then, the measure of your fathers. You serpents, you brood of vipers, how are you to escape being sentenced to hell?*

Matthew 23:29-33 (ESV)

These rebukes were for the governing body in his day. He not only rebuked them with words, he also became physically violent in the Temple with the money changers. Jesus was so enraged that he came in with a whip of cords and drove them out. That's confrontation. That's exposing corruption.

*In the Temple, he found those selling oxen, sheep, pigeons, and the money-changers sitting there. And making a whip of cords, he drove them all out of the Temple, with the sheep and oxen. And he poured out the money changers' coins and overturned their tables. And he told those who sold the pigeons, "Take these things away; do not make my Father's house a house of trade."*

John 2:14-16 (ESV)

Why did Jesus hate the money changers? According to Bill O'Reilly, in *Killing Jesus*:

The money changers exchanged the Roman coins adorned with images of living things such as gods or with portraits of the emperor into shekels, the standard currency of Jerusalem. Also known as the "Temple tax coin," the shekel is disparaged by many pilgrims because it is the only form of money acceptable for paying the annual tax (notice the word tax again) for purchasing animals for ritual slaughter. The money changers demand unfair exchange rates for the privilege of turning local money into shekels. The Temple High Priest also profits from this scam. When the Temple loans money to peasants who need help paying their taxes, the interest rates are exorbitant. Ledger sheets within the Temple's grand vaults keep a tally of all debts, and those who cannot repay suffer severe indignities: the loss of a home, loss of land and livestock, and eventually life as a debt slave or membership in the "unclean" class. The slums of lower Jerusalem are packed with families who were driven from their land because they could not repay the money they borrowed from the Temple. During Passover, as many as four million Jews make their way to Jerusalem each year. This means more income for the local shop owners and innkeepers, but the Temple priest and their Roman master get most of the profit through taxation and money changing. Even more money is made when the poor must buy a lamb or dove for the mandatory Passover sacrifice. If a priest should inspect the animal or bird and find even a single blemish, the sacrifice will be deemed unclean and the peasant will be forced to buy another.[32]

The Temple leaders profited through mandatory taxation and people lost their livelihoods. Jesus didn't ignore the injustice. When Jesus overturned the tables, he focused on the corruption of the money changers that the Sanhedrin manipulated. He loved the sheep of his pasture, but he ripped apart the bloodthirsty wolves of usury. He was addressing the corruption of his day and ministering to the poor, sick, and the lost. He led by example and did not fear the governing authorities. He followed his father's voice, which would lead Jesus to expose the corruption, not ignore it.

Today, Christians ignore the injustice in our communities by saying that Jesus wasn't interested in civil government and that the church is to focus on the Kingdom of God. If we are Christ's followers, the Kingdom of God is within us and by the example set by our Lord and Savior, let's expose the deeds of darkness and advance his kingdom until he comes.

# 14

# Apostle Paul and Romans

THE BOOK OF ROMANS is as deep as it is wide, delving into many themes, including God's role in civil government and how the Christian community should interact with governing authorities.

Paul gets right to the heart of the matter in Romans.

*Let every person be subject to the governing authorities. For there is no authority except from God, and those that exist have been instituted by God. Therefore, whoever resists the authorities resists what God has appointed, and those who resist will incur judgment. For rulers are not a terror to good conduct, but to bad. Would you have no fear of the one who is in authority? Then do what is good, and you will receive his approval, for he is God's servant for your good. But if you do wrong, be afraid, for he does not bear the sword in vain. For he is the servant of God, an avenger who carries out God's wrath on the wrongdoer. Therefore, one must be in subjection, not only to avoid God's wrath but also for the sake of conscience. For because of this you also pay taxes, for the authorities are ministers of God, attending to this very thing. Pay to all what is owed to them: taxes to whom taxes are owed, revenue to whom revenue is owed, respect to whom respect is owed, honor to whom honor is owed.*

Romans 13:1-7 (ESV)

The context of these words is revealing. At the time this book was written, Rome was the absolute ruling power of the known world and Caesar was considered a god. According to N.T. Wright,

The emperor was the *kyrios*, the lord of the world, the one who claimed the allegiance and loyalty of subjects throughout his wide empire. When he came in person to pay a state visit to a colony or province, the word for his royal presence was parousia.[33]

At first glance, it appears that Romans 13 is about quiet submission to a pagan ruler, no questions asked, just be still and keep your head down. But further study reveals that the Apostle Paul was really promoting the lordship of Jesus Christ—the true God and ruler of all the earth.

Paul begins the letter to the Romans by stating emphatically that Jesus is the one true God, and that he should be worshiped above all. Some theologians believe that Paul was actually confronting the rule of Caesar by claiming allegiance to Jesus Christ and pointing to his divine authority and headship. In Romans 1:17 Paul writes that he is not ashamed of the gospel of Christ because it is power, the power of God. As Christians, we follow Paul's example in pledging our allegiance to our Lord and Savior Jesus. Indeed, the gospel of Matthew tells us the same.

> *And Jesus came and said to them, "All authority in heaven and on earth has been given to me."*

> Matthew 28:18 (ESV)

Because of this authority, Paul boldly states to Roman Christians—citizens of the most powerful nation on earth—that "there is no authority except from God, and those that exist have been instituted by God" (Romans 13:1).

There are several points to observe in Romans 13.

In verses 3-4, Paul is saying that Roman rulers functioned as God's servant, bearing God's sword and that they need not be feared by citizens doing good. And yet, the Roman world was pagan and worshiped several other gods, none of whom were Jesus. Most of the people worshiped Caesar—a mere man in God's eyes but a deity to the masses. How then could these Roman officials be servants of God when they didn't honor God? The answer is that Paul was not referring to specific officials but the authority they carried. Their authority was from God, and Paul was sending a message both to Roman Christians and to those in authority: All who carry God's authority will have to answer to the One who gave it.

Governmental authority is given by God for the sake of peace and order. The underlying message of Romans 13 was that as long as the governing officials were operating justly, Christians were to obey them. However, if they were asked to denounce their faith, Scripture is clear that they cannot and should not deny the One who saved them, and so they should obey God rather than man.

It wasn't easy living in Rome as a Christian. The Church had to be on its guard at all times. And yet, note the level of governmental engagement to which Paul exhorted the Church. "Pay to all what is owed to them: taxes to whom taxes are owed, revenue to whom revenue is owed, respect to whom respect is owed, honor to whom honor is owed" (Romans 13:7). This is a model for engaging the world as active citizens, not hiding away in darkness waiting for the end. Roman Christians were being instructed to be fully present in the place God had ordained them to live.

We find this principle throughout Scripture. Whatever condition the Church finds itself in, it is to obey the Lord and live.

> *Build houses and settle down; plant gardens and eat what they produce. Marry and have sons and daughters; find wives for your sons and give your daughters in marriage, so that they too may have sons and daughters. Increase in number there; do not decrease. Also, seek the peace and prosperity of the city to which I have carried you into exile. Pray to the Lord for it, because if it prospers, you too will prosper.*
>
> Jeremiah 29:5-7 (ESV)

Note the key phrase here: "seek the prosperity of the city to which I have carried you into exile." God ties the people's prosperity to that of the culture in which they find themselves.

Paul has similar words for his protégé Timothy.

*First of all, then, I urge that supplications, prayers, intercessions, and thanksgivings be made for all men, for kings and all who are in high positions, that we may lead a quiet and peaceable life, godly and dignified in every way.*

1 Timothy 2:1-2 (ESV)

Both Scriptures admonish participation and prayer from God's people for the regions in which they live, calling Christians to quiet, peaceful, productive lives through prayer and obedience.

Of course, this is not always possible. Remember that Paul was speaking to citizens of Rome—not only the most powerful but the most organized government at that time. Roman Christians lived at a time known as Pax Romana, a period of relative peace and stability achieved by the Roman Empire from 27 BC to 180 AD. Knowing the conditional nature of this peace may have been on Paul's mind when he wrote in chapter 12:

*If possible, so far as it depends on you, live peaceably with all.*

Romans 12:18

It would not always be like that. Indeed, the same Rome to which Paul urged loyalty would be the Rome that, in the near future, savagely persecuted Christians through ritualized torture as public spectacle. Indeed, the Church continues to suffer persecution and affliction today. This is why the underlying principle is still to pray and obey and do good as much as we possibly can, even to the point of blessing our persecutors.

*Bless those who persecute you; bless and do not curse them.*

Romans 12:14

The key to Romans 13 is engagement, participating in society, living by the rules, and honoring authority. How much more blessings would come on a nation if more Christians became part of the political process and began to enter places of government?

Governmental positions of authority are given by the God we serve and obey. Following the pattern of Scripture, Christians should be positioned in all types and levels of government to rule, to do good, and to influence many.

The Church needs to enter every place of society. Instead of just praying for ungodly leaders to make good and godly decisions, let's pray for the Church to rise up and possess these leadership places in our government. The Church has the things of God: knowledge, mercy, peace, and forgiveness. We are the people who will rule well and bring stability to their nation.

# 15

# Peter, Paul and Civil Authority

*Obeying God Versus Obeying the Government*

WHEN THE SUBJECT OF SUBMISSION comes up for discussion among Christians, the opinions vary depending on a person's interpretation of Romans13:1-6 and 1 Peter 2:13.

> *Let every person be subject to the governing authorities. For there is no authority except from God, and those that exist have been instituted by God. Therefore whoever resists the authorities resists what God has appointed, and those who resist will incur judgment. For rulers are not a terror to good conduct, but to bad. Would you have no fear of the one who is in authority? Then do what is good, and you will receive his approval, for he is God's servant for your good. But if you do wrong, be afraid, for he does not bear the sword in vain. For he is the servant of God, an avenger who carries out God's wrath on the wrongdoer. Therefore one must be in subjection, not only to avoid God's wrath but also for the sake of conscience. For because of this you also pay taxes, for the authorities are ministers of God, attending to this very thing.*

> Romans 13:1-6 (ESV)

> *Be subject for the Lord's sake to every human institution, whether it be to the emperor as supreme, or to governors as sent by him to punish those who do evil and to praise those*

*who do good. For this is the will of God, that by doing good you should put to silence the ignorance of foolish people. Live as people who are free, not using your freedom as a cover-up for evil, but living as servants of God. Honor everyone. Love the brotherhood. Fear God. Honor the emperor.*

1Peter 2:13-16 (ESV)

Civil government was created to punish evil-doers and reward the just. Paul and Peter are clear on the purpose of civil government in both passages. The Lord desires submission to civil authority. But the questions are:

- How far should our subjection go?
- What happens when the civil government goes too far?
- What happens when civil government rewards the evil doers and punishes those who do good or persecutes those who obey the laws?

There are precedents in the Bible to follow if the civil government crosses scriptural boundaries.

Paul and Peter were Apostles of our Lord and Savior, Christ Jesus. They were called to establish the beginnings of Christianity and the Church of the living God. They were fathers and shepherds releasing wisdom to the saints with instructions on conducting and living their daily lives in a system that did not understand or favor Christ's followers. Their teachings are wisdom for believers and law-abiding citizens.

Let's look at the Apostle Peter first. Remember that Peter was subject to the same authorities that crucified Jesus. Julian Spriggs says:

The Pharisees and Sadducees were not just religious leaders. They were also the political leaders of Israel during Jesus' time. Israel was called Judah at the time, renamed Judea by the Romans. The Romans did not run everything in Judea, not even close. As long as the Jews paid their taxes and didn't revolt, Rome had little interest in their internal affairs. It was the normal Roman practice to leave most of the government running to local leaders. In Judea, this was the Sanhedrin, dominated by the Sadducees and ruled by the High Priest. In return for their support for the Roman rule, the Sadducees kept their wealth and privileged position secure. The Sanhedrin were the overseers of the chief legislative, judicial, and religious functions. Members of the Sanhedrin were the equivalent of the congress and senators that represent us today."[34]

From Acts:

*Peter was therefore kept in prison, but constant prayer was offered to God for him by the church. And when Herod was about to bring him out, that night Peter was sleeping, bound with two chains between two soldiers; and the guards before the door were keeping the prison. Now behold, an angel of the Lord stood by him, and a light shone in the prison; and he struck Peter on the side and raised him up, saying, "Arise quickly!" And his chains fell off his hands. Then the angel said to him, "Gird yourself and tie on your sandals"; and so he did. And he said to him, "Put on your garment and follow me." So he went out and followed him, and did not know that what was done by the angel was real, but thought he was seeing a vision. When they were past the first and the second guard posts, they came to the iron gate that leads to the city, which opened to them of its own accord; and they went out and went down one street, and immediately the angel departed from him.*

*And when Peter had come to himself, he said, "Now I know for certain that the Lord has sent his angel, and has delivered me from the hand of Herod and from all the expectation of the Jewish people.*

*Then, as soon as it was day, there was no small stir among the soldiers about what had become of Peter. But when Herod had searched for him and not found him, he examined the guards and commanded that they should be put to death.*

Acts 12:5-11,18-19 (NKJV)

Peter was delivered from prison—from the civil authorities who ordered him there—and it was no small feat. In fact, Herod put to death the guards who kept watch over Peter. According to this passage, the civil government crossed the boundaries by imprisoning Peter.

*Now many signs and wonders were regularly done among the people by the hands of the apostles. And they were all together in Solomon's Portico. None of the rest dared join them, but the people held them in high esteem. And more than ever believers were added to the Lord, multitudes of both men and women, so that they even carried out the sick into the streets and laid them on cots and mats, that as Peter came by at least his shadow might fall on some of them. The people also gathered from the towns around Jerusalem, bringing the sick and those afflicted with unclean spirits, and they were all healed.*

*But the high Priest rose up, and all who were with him (that is, the party of the Sadducees), and filled with jealousy they arrested the apostles and put them in the public prison. But during the night an angel of the Lord opened the prison doors and brought them out, and said, "Go and stand in the temple and speak to the people all the words of this Life." And when they heard this, they entered the temple at daybreak and began to teach.*

*Now when the high Priest came, and those who were with him, they called together the council, all the senate of the people of Israel, and sent to the prison to have them brought.*

*But when the officers came, they did not find them in prison, so they returned and reported, "We found the prison securely locked and the guards standing at the doors, but when we opened them, we found no one inside." Now when the captain of the temple and the chief priests heard these words, they were greatly perplexed about them, wondering what this would come to. And someone came and told them, "Look! The men whom you put in prison are standing in the temple and teaching the people." Then the captain with the officers went and brought them, but not by force, for they were afraid of being stoned by the people.*

*And when they had brought them, they set them before the council. And the high Priest questioned them, saying, "We strictly charged you not to teach in this name, yet here you have filled Jerusalem with your teaching, and you intend to bring this man's blood upon us." But Peter and the apostles answered, "We must obey God rather than men. The God of our fathers raised Jesus, whom you killed by hanging him on a tree. God exalted him at his right hand as Leader and Savior to give repentance to Israel and forgiveness of sins. And we are witnesses to these things, and so is the Holy Spirit, whom God has given to those who obey him."*

*When they heard this, they were enraged and wanted to kill them.*

Acts 5:12-33 (ESV)

Now, remember the authority of the high Priest in Peter's day. Bill O'Reilly states in Killing Jesus:

The Sanhedrin is the ultimate Jewish religious court, a body of men even more powerful than the tetrarch Antipas. And within this chamber, Caiaphas, the High Priest born into a

109

centuries-long lineage of wealthy Temple priests, holds the ultimate authority.[35]

This authority imprisoned the Apostles and tried to get them to stop preaching the Gospel. They even wanted to kill them, but God had another plan. When the high priest strictly charged them to stop teaching in the name of Jesus, their response was, "We must obey God rather than men."

As Christians, this is our foundation. We must obey God first. God is our supreme ruler and the source of all living beings. He is our king, judge, and lawgiver. He is our father. Our foundation and precedent is based on this understanding of who God is.

Next, we see two visible actions of the Apostle Paul dealing with civil government. The subject in the following passages deals with citizenship, particularly the Roman citizen.

Victor Hanson Davis's book, *The Dying Citizen*, says:

> Citizenship came late to civilization, and citizenship began with the Greeks and then expanded with the Romans. The Roman civics (civil, civic, civilization, etc.) or citizen was the beneficiary of rights codified in an extensive body of law. Legal protection for the civics against arbitrary arrest, confiscation, or taxation ensured the value of Citizenship. Indeed, later, throughout the Roman-controlled Mediterranean, echoed the republican-era boast civics Romanus sum-"I am a Roman Citizen." The speaker, if he was so fortunate as to live inside the boundaries of Rome's growing dominions, was entitled to rights that transcended those of both transient foreigners and mere permanent residents within Roman lands. Empowerment was again the key; give a citizen equality under the law, freedom and economic viability, and his talents will bloom and enrich the state at large.[36]

The phrase, "I am a Roman Citizen" contained authority and weight in civil and jurisdiction power. The Apostle Paul referred to this authority when needed.

> *But when it was day, the magistrates sent the police, saying, "let those men go." And the jailer reported these words to Paul, saying, "The magistrates have sent to let you go. Therefore, come out now and go in peace. But Paul said to them, "They have beaten us publicly, uncondemned, men who are Roman Citizens, and have thrown us into prison, and do the now throw us out secretly? NO-Let them come themselves and take us out." The police reported these words to the magistrates, and they were afraid when they heard that they were Roman citizens. So they came and apologized to them and they took them out and asked them to leave the city.*

> Acts 16:35-39 (ESV)

> *The tribune ordered him to be brought into the barracks, saying that he should be examined by flogging, to find out why they were shouting against him like this, but when they had stretched him out for the whips, Paul said to the centurion who was standing by, "Is it lawful for you to flog a man who is a Roman citizen and condemned? When the centurion heard this, he went to the tribune and said to him, "What are you about to do? For this man is a Roman citizen." So the tribune came and said to him, "Tell me, are you a Roman citizen?" And he said, "Yes" The tribune answered, "I bought my citizenship for a large sum." Paul said, "But I am a citizen by birth." So those who were about to examine him withdrew from him immediately, and the tribune also was afraid.*

> Acts 22: 24-29 (ESV)

In both passages, Paul calls upon his citizenship to protect himself and confront civil authority. He was a natural-born citizen of Rome, and Paul knew his authority both as a citizen of Rome and as an apostle. In the Apostle Paul's writings, he used motifs, symbols, and analogies. One of those analogies was the word *citizenship.*

> *Remember that at that time you were separate from Christ, excluded from citizenship in Israel and foreigners to the covenants of the promise, without hope and without God in the world. But now in Christ Jesus you who once were far away have been brought near by the blood of Christ.*
>
> *Consequently, you are no longer foreigners and strangers, but fellow citizens with God's people and also members of his household.*

Ephesians 2:12-13, 19 (NIV)

Apart from Christ, Christians were excluded from Citizenship in Israel. But now, presently, we are fellow citizens with God's people.

> *But our citizenship is in heaven, and from it, we await a Savior, the Lord Jesus Christ.*

Philippians 3:20 (ESV)

Citizenship did not originate with the Greeks or the Romans. Citizenship came from the heart of God and was established when he set Israel apart as his own peculiar nation. Without God, we are excluded from heaven's citizenship. Which virtually means being an outsider to the promises, blessings, and covenant protections of relationship with Almighty God.

Presently, we who are Christians are fellow citizens with God's people. What does this mean? Christians cannot understand the depth of being a citizen of God's kingdom, both now and in the future, without understanding what it means to be a citizen on earth.

Here's the beauty of being a citizen in the United States and other Western nations. Romans 13:1 (ESV) says: "there is no authority except from God, and those that exist have been instituted by God."

In the United States, civil rulers and leaders receive their positions of authority through the citizen's vote. Therefore, the citizens are the ones with authority from God. The elected officials are in office because of the people who vote and don't vote. The Lord established that the voter would determine who rules over the United States. Unfortunately, the citizens, including Christians, are abdicating their authority and giving these ruling offices to immoral, depraved, and unjust people—people full of greed and lust for power. The government is corrupt because the church is not participating even at the most manageable level—the vote.

As much as possible, we are to live as law-abiding citizens and lead quiet and peaceable lives. Many of the ills brought on by our government are because citizens will not take their rightful place and vote for righteous men and women who are called to civil government. Because of the church's lack of participation and not understanding their governmental responsibility, we now have leaders at the highest level in nations calling good "evil" and evil "good." If the church in mass numbers prayed and voted, we would experience different outcomes in everyday laws.

The United States is a blessed nation, giving the Gospel to millions worldwide and releasing religious freedom of expression to everyone. This religious freedom is a gift from God and must be protected, or it will be lost. The loss is not by the will of God, but by the disobedience of citizens not taking proper responsibility to hold on to it.

The church is to obey God first and be responsible for things God has entrusted to her in every generation.

# Volume II

# How the Church Can Participate in Government

# Introduction to Volume II

IN VOLUME I, WE ASKED WHY THE CHURCH SHOULD BE INVOLVED in government. In answer to that query, we discovered that government involvement is part of a Christian's biblical heritage. Throughout Scripture, we see the Lord's movement and careful occupation upon his people to effect change on the government in every dispensation.

Having answered the first question—why—we will now address how the Church can participate in government. Simply put, the most predominant way the Church can participate in government is by being present.

Recall roll call in school when the teacher called your name and you raised your hand to show you were there. The opposite of "present" is "absent." A person cannot participate in class if they are absent. They cannot acquire knowledge or participate in the class. Absence is an empty space that needs to be filled.

The problem with empty spaces is two-fold.

It either means that others need to work harder to fill the void that someone else should be filling. Or the space never gets filled at all, and darkness prevails. Like a neglected piece of soil, weeds will grow and choke out the good plants that are trying to grow.

> *I went by the field belonging to a lazy man, by a vineyard belonging to a senseless person. There it was, overgrown with thistles, the ground covered with thorns, its stone wall collapsed.*

> Proverbs 24:30-31 (ISV)

We all know the home of a sluggard. It's the ramshackle house on the corner with trash spewed everywhere. There are broken-down cars in the driveway, overgrown grass in the yard, and children running around with bare feet and dirty faces. Meanwhile, the mother sits on the porch with a beer in one hand and a cigarette in the other. She's on the phone calling the police because the last man in the house ransacked the place and stole her rent money.

This is an absence of authority in the extreme—when the person who is called to occupy the space goes AWOL and no one is left in charge.

> *When the righteous triumph, there is great elation; but when the wicked rise to power, people go into hiding.*

Proverbs 28:12

Christians who are present—not absent—can pay attention to governmental issues, ward off the darkness, and keep the weeds from their sphere of influence in our society. Clearly, this is what Jesus meant in this parable:

> *"You are the salt of the world. But if the salt should lose its taste, how can it be made salty again? It's good for nothing but to be thrown out and trampled on by people."*

Matthew 5:13 (ISV)

The Lord sends us out as the salt of the earth, but why salt? What led him to choose that metaphor? Considering its importance, we need an extensive biblical meaning of salt. According to Abarim Publications,

In the old world, raw salt was highly sought after (our words salary and sale come from the Latin word for salt). Its bottom line is that it stops decay and disintegration; it keeps together what is supposed to be together by arresting the forces that want to tear things apart.29

The website also talks about how salt's applications fall into distinct categories:

1. Salt draws water and blood out of butchered meat, while fungi and bacteria either die or become inactive. Salt also slows down the oxidation of fats, which is what causes meat to go rancid. Salt stops the decay of something dead.

118

2. Salt disinfects a wound.
3. Salt was used to "disinfect" people who were deemed so infectious to the culture at large that they had to be cut away like putrid flesh from a wounded body. The area was to be turned into a "burning waste, unsown and unproductive," that "no grass grows in it" (Deuteronomy 29:22). In the Bible, two clear instances of this deep cleaning are recorded. (See Psalm 107:34, Jeremiah 17:6, Isaiah 34:9, Zephaniah 2:9.)
4. Salt kills impurities similar to fire. "For everyone will be salted with fire" (Mark 9:49).

In the Deuteronomic School, Moshe Weinfeld submits, "razing and burning of a city and its sowing with salt and brimstone seems to have been the conventional punishment for breach of treaty."[37]

he goes on to cite the records of several known Assyrian kings who resorted to that practice after such a transgression. But note that salt is not just a symbol of death; it's the symbol of death of that which is rotten. As such, it is a symbol of healing and regeneration of that which was contaminated (2 Kings 2:20-21).

Throughout the ages, entire wars were fought over salt, and note the similarity between our noun חלמ (*melah*), meaning salt, and the word המחלמ (*milhama*), meaning battle or war. The latter comes from the root מחל (*laham*), which either means to wage war or to eat. It's part of the name of Jesus' birthplace: Bethlehem. When Jesus says: "You are the salt of the earth," he doesn't just mean to say what a fine condiment we are.

Salt, therefore, is an instrument of trial and judgment. It is fatal to death, sin, and sinners, and is life to the saved. The lake of fire (ref. Revelation 19:20) is, by implication, similar to a lake of salt. Note that while sin's ultimate destiny is the "depth of the sea," the surface of the Dead Sea—the saltiest body of water on earth—is the lowest point on earth (ref. Micah 7:19).

The meaning of salt has ties to battle as well. If the church is the salt of the earth, occupying a governmental role must be viewed through the lens of waging war, judging, and cleansing with God's Word. When a person decides to participate in government, they become a fiery salt shaker for the Kingdom of God, one that will purge and heal every issue it engages.

With a better understanding of Jesus' parable, we begin to see that the Church is salt to civil government, seeking that which can be accomplished on a deeper level. For instance, consider a Christian who runs for a political office. If that person takes hold of their position and responsibility by faith, the salt within them will begin the process of purifying, preserving, and regenerating the governmental functions they are fulfilling. It will now be possible to stop decay, disinfect the wounds, and heal the contamination present in that office.

Of course, not every person is called to the same levels of civil government, but there are specific instructions that are given to the Church as a whole. Romans 13 is an extensive treatise on the Church's role in civil government, describing the Church's role with beauty and order.

Let everyone be subject to the governing authorities, for there is no authority except that which God has established. The authorities that exist have been established by God. Consequently, whoever rebels against the authority is rebelling against what God has instituted, and those who do so will bring judgment on themselves. For rulers hold no terror for those who do right, but for those who do wrong. Do you want to be free from fear of the one in authority? Then do what is right and you will be commended. For the one in authority is God's servant for your good. But if you do wrong, be afraid, for rulers do not bear the sword for no reason. They are God's servants, agents of wrath to bring punishment on the wrongdoer. Therefore, it is necessary to submit to the authorities, not only because of possible punishment but also as a matter of conscience.

*This is also why you pay taxes, for the authorities are God's servants, who give their full time to governing. Give to everyone what you owe them: If you owe taxes, pay taxes; if*

*revenue, then revenue; if respect, then respect; if honor, then
honor.*

Romans 13:1-7 (ESV)

Consider Paul's key words: "The authorities that exist have been
established by God." They are the foundation for understanding the
importance of government. If a person believes in God and his eternal
pathways, the understanding that authority exists because of God is the
first step to wisdom. However, it begs the question: How can I be more
involved?

Obedience to civil authority is important. Our actions are powerful
displays of the glory of God, but it goes deeper than that. Honoring a
ruler because of their position in government is a witness to the gospel.
Paying our taxes is a witness to the gospel. Respecting the rule of law
is a witness to the gospel.

Over the years, I have heard many fellow believers say that they just
want to serve God. Those who voice this desire typically look to church
ministries for fruitful service. And while some find fulfillment there,
others are disappointed trying to figure out the call of God on their
lives. Yes, serving in church ministries is important. However, civil
rulers are also servants of God. They carry power and authority—the
ability to change society for the good of all mankind.

In the following chapters, we will explore the diverse ways a
Christian can serve the Lord in the world through governing in various
institutions and layers of government.

# 16

# <u>Prayer</u>

ON DECEMBER 1944, AT THE HEIGHT OF WORLD WAR II, General Patton called upon his chief of staff Colonel Paul D. Hawkins and Chaplain O'Neill of the Third Army. According to Hawkins, this is how Patton called upon the chaplain to pray:

> <u>General Patton</u>: Chaplain, I want you to publish a prayer for good weather. I'm tired of these soldiers having to fight mud and floods as well as Germans. See if we can't get God to work on our side.

> <u>Chaplain O'Neill</u>: Sir, it's going to take a pretty thick rug for that kind of praying.

> <u>General Patton</u>: I don't care if it takes the flying carpet. I want the praying done.

> <u>Chaplain O'Neill</u>: Yes, sir. May I say, General, that it usually isn't a customary thing among men of my profession to pray for clear weather to kill fellow men.

> <u>General Patton</u>: Chaplain, are you teaching me theology or are you the Chaplain of the Third Army? I want a prayer.

> <u>Chaplain O'Neill</u>: Yes, sir.[38]

In the book, *War As I Knew It*, by George S. Patton this prayer was distributed to every soldier in the U.S. Third Army:

> Almighty God and most merciful Father, we humbly beseech Thee, of Thy great goodness, to restrain these immoderate rains with which we have had to contend. Grant us fair weather for Battle. Graciously hearken to us as soldiers who

call upon Thee that, armed with Thy power, we may advance from victory to victory, and crush the oppression and wickedness of our enemies, and establish Thy justice among men and nations. Amen.[39]

The skies cleared within twenty-four hours. A week of perfect weather ensued, allowing the Allies to advance toward the Rhine. Patton was ecstatic and gave Chaplain O'Neill a Bronze Star.

As a young girl, I loved to play chess. While concentrating on every move, trying to figure out the best way to maneuver around the board, I noticed that the first pieces to be maneuvered would be the pawns. They were used to get closer to the king; it was always about taking out the king. In chess, when a person takes out the opponent's highest authority, their side wins. There have been many theories comparing chess to war. In war, there are tactics, strategies, defense, counterattacks, and breakthroughs. Every soldier has a vital role just as every piece on the chess board has a position. In the wrong position, a knight or bishop is powerless; in the right position, a lowly pawn can take out a king. Strategically, a pawn can support a stronger piece to take out the king, or the pawn can go directly and take it out itself. In Christianity, the pawn is the person engaged in spiritual warfare, prayers, and petitions. Often unheralded because their work is unseen, they are indispensable.

Years ago, I was invited to a women's breakfast at a local church in our city. The speaker was a state senator here in my home state of Washington. She had faithfully served our district for many years. One of her statements to those in attendance was this: "If Christians knew the many things that we are called to vote on every day, they would be on their knees crying out to God for wisdom for their elected officials." There are many paths that a person can take to participate in government. But there is one specific instruction given to the Church, and it is asked of every believer, and that is to pray.

*I urge, then, first of all, that petitions, prayers, intercession and thanksgiving be made for all people—for kings and all those in authority, that we may live peaceful and quiet lives in all godliness and holiness.*

1 Timothy 2:1-2

The reasons above are simple enough. We are asked to pray for government in order to live peaceful, quiet lives. The opposite of peace is war. So, praying for governmental leaders will push back the warfare.

Of course, God would not tell us to pray if it were not necessary. But this begs the question: Is the future fixed or fluid? What impact do our actions have on the world and the lives around us? The answer, I believe, is in the scriptural examples of future outcomes based on choices made by people. Indeed, the evidence for cause and effect of certain outcomes is abundant. According to Michael Saia in his book, *Why Pray?:*

> The idea of the absolute predestination of all events is not biblical. The notion that the Bible teaches this doctrine is based on false assumptions about certain passages. Because some events were predestined by God, this does not mean every event in history was determined ahead of time. If all choices are fixed, then there is no free will, love is a sham, and any relationship with God is worthless.

Consider these scriptural examples Saia references:

*But if they had stood in My council, then they would have announced My words to My people and would have turned them back from their evil way and from the evil of their deeds.*

Jeremiah 23:22 (ESV)

Notice the words, "If they had…they would…."

*If only you had paid attention to My commandments!*

*Then your well-being would have been like a river, and your righteousness like the waves of the sea.*

Isaiah 48:18 (ESV)

Again, notice the words, "If only you had…then your well-being would have been…."

*The wisdom which none of the rulers of this age has understood; for if they had understood it, they would not have crucified the Lord of glory.*

1Corinthians 2:8 (NAS)

Notice the words, "If they had understood…they would not…."

*And you, Capernaum, will not be exalted to heaven, will you? you shall descend to Hades; for if the miracles had occurred in Sodom which occurred in you, it would have remained to this day.*

Matthew 11:23 (NAS)

Notice the words, "If the…it would…."
This last Scripture speaks to more than just the coming of the

*Lord; it is also about being watchful and alert in prayer for our leaders and rulers in this world. But be sure of this, that if the head of the house had known at what time of the night the thief was coming, he would have been on the alert and would not have allowed his house to be broken into.*

Matthew 24:43 (NAS)

Again, notice the cause-and-effect language: "If the head of the household had known…he would have been…."

There are many broken places in government that need to be restored. So looking back at our instruction, IF WE pray for authority, THEN WE will live a peaceable life. If we stay watchful and alert, we are protecting our house, city, and nation from being broken into.33[40]

126

Let's not forget the most famous Scripture of all,

*If my people, who are called by my name, will humble themselves and pray and seek my face and turn from their wicked ways, then I will hear from heaven, and I will forgive their sin and will heal their land.*

2Chronicles 7:14

Notice the words, "If my people…then I will…."

Another beautiful truth about our relationship with God is the ability to change God's mind. It's awe-inspiring to realize that we are heard by our creator and he considers our reasoning and our opinions when we pray. Consider Moses' interactions with God.

*The Lord said, "I have seen these people and they are a stiff-necked people...leave me alone so that my anger may burn against them and that I may destroy them. Then I will make you into a great nation." But Moses sought the favor of the Lord, "O Lord, why should your anger burn against your people, whom you brought out of Egypt with great power and a mighty hand? Why should the Egyptians say, 'It was with evil intent that he brought them out, to kill them in the mountains and to wipe them off the face of the earth'? Turn from your fierce anger; relent and do not bring disaster on your people. Remember your servants Abraham, Isaac and Israel, to whom you swore by your own self: 'I will make your descendants as numerous as the stars in the sky and I will give your descendants all this land I promised them, and it will be their inheritance forever.'"*

Exodus 32:9-13

*Then the Lord changed his mind and did not bring on his people the disaster he had threatened.*

Exodus 32:14

Moses reasoned with the Lord, explaining why destroying his people was a bad idea. In fact, he gave the Lord three specific reasons, showing that his entreaty to God was well thought out. This is not a symbolic story. If we can believe Scripture, Moses changed God's mind.

Consider how Abraham reasoned with the Lord about the destruction of Sodom.

> *The men turned away and went toward Sodom, but Abraham remained standing before the LORD.*
>
> *Then Abraham approached him and said: "Will you sweep away the righteous with the wicked? What if there are fifty righteous people in the city? Will you really sweep it away and not spare the place for the sake of the fifty righteous people in it? Far be it from you to do such a thing—to kill the righteous with the wicked, treating the righteous and the wicked alike. Far be it from you! Will not the Judge of all the earth do right?"*
>
> *The LORD said, "If I find fifty righteous people in the city of Sodom, I will spare the whole place for their sake."*
>
> *Then Abraham spoke up again: "Now that I have been so bold as to speak to the Lord, though I am nothing but dust and ashes, what if the number of the righteous is five less than fifty? Will you destroy the whole city for lack of five people?"*
>
> *"If I find forty-five there," he said, "I will not destroy it."*
>
> *Once again he spoke to him, "What if only forty are found there?"*
>
> *he said, "For the sake of forty, I will not do it."*
>
> *Then he said, "May the Lord not be angry, but let me speak. What if only thirty can be found there?"*
>
> *he answered, "I will not do it if I find thirty there."*

*Abraham said, "Now that I have been so bold as to speak to the Lord, what if only twenty can be found there?"*

*he said, "For the sake of twenty, I will not destroy it."*

*Then he said, "May the Lord not be angry, but let me speak just once more. What if only ten can be found there?"*

*he answered, "For the sake of ten, I will not destroy it."*

*When the LORD had finished speaking with Abraham, he left, and Abraham returned home.*

Genesis 8:22-33

Abraham was able to get God to change his mind several times.

Of course, we'll never know if the Lord could have been talked out of destroying Sodom to save one righteous person. The point is that God and Abraham engaged in dialogue, and God changed his mind.

One more recorded example of a person changing God's mind is found in Amos 7.

*This is what the Sovereign Lord showed me: he was preparing swarms of locusts after the king's share had been harvested and just as the late crops were coming up. When they had stripped the land clean, I cried out, "Sovereign Lord, forgive! How can Jacob survive? he is so small!"*

*So the Lord relented.*

*"This will not happen," the Lord said.*

*This is what the Sovereign Lord showed me: The Sovereign Lord was calling for judgment by fire; it dried up the great deep and devoured the land. Then I cried out, "Sovereign Lord, I beg you, stop! How can Jacob survive? he is so small!"*

*So the Lord relented.*

*"This will not happen either," the Sovereign Lord said.*

Amos 7:1-6

All Amos had to do to change God's mind was to argue that Jacob was small and would not survive if the Lord destroyed the land. It didn't take much reasoning with God. So, was the Lord just looking for someone to ask him to stop? It's hard to tell. What we do know from these examples, however, is that God responds to prayers and petitions, and everything is on the table.

Some people are called to intercession for the government and its officials. This is no easy task. Intercession is deep and takes much time and energy. The prophet Daniel was a governmental intercessor. His actions support the view that the future is not fixed, but instead responds to our involvement.

*In the first year of Darius son of Xerxes (a Mede by descent), who was made ruler over the Babylonian kingdom in the first year of his reign, I, Daniel, understood from the Scriptures, according to the word of the LORD given to Jeremiah the prophet, that the desolation of Jerusalem would last seventy years. So I turned to the Lord God and pleaded with him in prayer and petition, in fasting, and in sackcloth and ashes. I prayed to the LORD my God and confessed.*

Daniel 9:1-4

Consider the evidence. If the will of the Lord is predetermined, why was Daniel so concerned about praying, fasting, and repenting for his people and his nation? In Daniel 10, Daniel set himself to pray for twenty-one days. Derek Prince, in his book, Praying for the Government, gives a fascinating take on Daniel's intercession.

Daniel set himself to pray for twenty-one days with special earnestness for divine intervention on behalf of his people. At the end of this period, an angel came with a revelation that was the answer to his prayers.

The angel told Daniel: "From the first day that you set your heart to understand and to humble yourself before your God, your words were heard; and I come because of your words." Daniel prayed for twenty-one days, yet his prayer was heard the first day. Why did he have to wait twenty-one days for the answer? In verse 13, the angel went on to give the reason: "But the prince of the kingdom of Persia withstood me twenty-one days; and behold, Michael, one of the chief princes, came to help me." This "prince of the kingdom of Persia" was not a human being. These events did not take place on the human plane. It was an angel who brought the message, and it was an angel who opposed the angelic messenger. Another angel, Michael, came to the assistance of the first angel. This was a spiritual warfare of angels in the heavenlies. Notice, it was what happened on earth that decided the course of events in heaven. This is a tremendous truth. Nothing happened until Daniel started to pray. It was Daniel's prayers that got the angel through, not the angel that got Daniel through. Daniel got the angel through! If only God's people would see that the issues are settled by us. They are not even settled by the angels. Revelation 12:11 tells us: "They"—God's people on earth—"overcame him"—Satan—"by the blood of the Lamb, and by the word of their testimony." We are the decisive factor in the affairs of the universe. I am not exaggerating one bit. If Daniel had not prayed, things would never have happened in heaven. He had to pray for twenty-one days to get the answer. What delayed the answer? This was not because Daniel did not pray according to the will of God. There was nothing wrong with his prayer. Satan, in the person of the prince of the kingdom of Persia, was the reason for the delay.34[41]

The future is not fixed. Everything is negotiable with God. Prayer is the leverage that we possess to change the world in which we live.

How and what we pray is equally important. First of all, a prayer can't be in a void. Being specific as possible increases faith and opens the deep heart. It's a good idea to know the names of the leaders in civil authority. What is the mayor's name? What does he or she stand for? What are the names of the people on the local school board? What kind of decisions are they making for the children in their district? Is the state legislature trying to pass ordinances and laws affecting religious liberties or personal liberties? Knowing what's on the docket and what's being debated in session gives more substance to our prayers and intercession. Praying for wisdom is good, but specific directed prayer is better. In Scripture we see Jesus saying, "What can I do for you?" He asks us to give specific requests. To get started on your prayer journey, here is a website with several guides. These guides are a foundation. Use them, and then personalize your prayers according to what is happening in your own city, region, and state.

When it comes to government, the one thing we are all asked to do is pray. Set aside some time, weekly or bi-weekly, to lift up our governmental officials and the issues concerning our time.[42]

# 17

# Vote

The vote is the most powerful instrument ever devised by man for breaking down injustice,

Lyndon Baines Johnson

IF THE STATEMENT ABOVE WAS BELIEVED AND PRACTICED, instead of half the American population voting, every person that could vote would vote. In the 1988 presidential election between George Bush and Michael Dukakis, 91,602,291 American people showed up to vote and 91,050,000 registered voters did not vote in that election. In the 2000 presidential election, after an intense recount process and the decision of the United States Supreme Court in Bush v. Gore, Governor George W. Bush officially won Florida's electoral votes by a margin of only 537 votes out of almost six million cast, and as a result, won the national presidential election.

Did you know that in 1840, women in the United States could not vote, sit on juries, or hold public office? In 1848, at a women's rights convention in Seneca Falls, women for the first time publicly demanded the right to vote. The media made fun of the women and the convention. It's stunning to think how hard women had to fight for the right to vote. In 1865, eight months after the Civil War ended, the government created the Thirteenth Amendment, which outlawed slavery. Then along came the Fourteenth Amendment with the right to citizenship and equal protection of the laws. But this still only applied to males over twenty-one. In came the Fifteenth Amendment that stated the right to vote could not be denied because of race, color, or whether they had been a slave. Oops! Only men apply, please!

Because the Fifteen Amendment didn't include women, it caused a rift in the women's suffrage movement. Some women were content that the African-American vote was won first. Others felt it was a sting to both black and white women alike. It took marches, protests, printed articles, and many organized meetings to bring the women's-right-to-vote campaign to the public. There were rifts between family members, especially between husbands and wives, and fathers and daughters. There was also an anti-suffragist movement led by women. These women argued that families would be destroyed because women would rebel against their husbands if they had the right to vote. There were major industries that fought hard against women voting. Cloth manufacturers employed huge numbers of women and were afraid that they would use their political power to fight for higher wages. Liquor manufacturers were against women voting because many women supported the temperance movement.

Then in 1878, twelve years after the first convention, a senator from California introduced an amendment for women's suffrage that became known as the "Susan B. Anthony Amendment." It didn't pass, and that amendment would be brought up before Congress every session for 42 years! Imagine for a moment being a woman living during these years. At that time, the media mocked women's suffrage leaders through political cartoons. In one cartoon, a woman voter was depicted as abandoning crying babies in the arms of her husband to go out and vote. These women were seen as rebellious troublemakers that wanted to ruin the fabric of society. The husbands of suffragists didn't have it easy, either. They were called henpecked and accused of tagging after the girls. The husbands were ostracized and told to go home and do the dishes. There were many heated augments between the husbands of suffragists and anti-suffragists. In 1917, a Quaker woman named Alice Paul even went to prison for picketing in front of the White House.

It finally came to a volatile head two years later when the Senate voted in favor of the Nineteenth Amendment, giving women the right to vote. In order for the bill to become law, however, three-quarters of the states had to ratify the amendment. The women of the suffrage movement had to convince thirty-six lawmakers to vote in favor of the amendment. It literally got down to one state—Tennessee—where it flew through the Senate but stalled in the House of Representatives. The governor called a special session to vote on the amendment. The fight for the vote in Tennessee became known as the "War of the Roses." Lawmakers in favor wore yellow; those opposed wore red. There was a deadlock vote of 48-48 and weeks of intense debate and lobbying. The suffragists wondered when their fifty-two-year battle would finally come to fruition.

On the day of the vote, Harry Burns-one of the youngest lawmakers in the House—entered the capitol building wearing a red rose. Everyone turned to Burns. With his red rose on his lapel, he spoke out loudly in favor of the amendment and reversed his opposing vote. Shock filled the room. The anti-suffragists were furious, but the suffragists cheered and rejoiced with all their hearts. It was such an intense battle that Harry fled to the attic of the state capitol and hid until the angry crowds dispersed. Some say he even crept onto a third-floor ledge to escape an angry mob of anti-suffragist lawmakers threatening to rough him up. He said later that the one reason he changed his vote at the last minute was that his mother asked him to.

One of the founding leaders of the suffrage movement, Carrie Chapman Catt, is quoted as saying,

> To get the word male in effect out of the Constitution cost the women of the country fifty-two years of pause-less campaigning.... During that time, they were forced to conduct fifty-six campaigns of referenda to male voters; 480 campaigns to get legislatures to submit suffrage amendments to voters; forty-seven campaigns to get state constitutional conventions to write woman suffrage into state constitutions; 277 campaigns to get state party conventions to include woman suffrage planks; thirty campaigns to get presidential party conventions to adopt woman suffrage planks in party

platforms; and nineteen campaigns with nineteen successive Congresses.

Millions of dollars were raised, mainly in small sums, and expended with economic care. Hundreds of women gave the accumulated possibilities of an entire lifetime, thousands gave years of their lives, hundreds of thousands gave constant interest and such aid as they could. It was a continuous, seemingly endless chain of activity. Young suffragists who helped forge the last links of that chain were not born when it began. Old suffragists who forged the first links were dead when it ended.[43]

Everything we have as rights and privileges has been fought and paid for by someone. The right to vote came through the perseverance of many women from Christian and other religious circles. To be effective, these people had to come out of their religious comfort zones and join a political movement. They had to choose to speak up for what they knew was right. This brought criticism and hardship. In their hearts, these women knew they were paving the way for justice. And yet, true and unending justice comes from one place—the heart of God the Father. The fact that God-fearing women took up the fight, leaving their church pews and the comfort of their places in society, has given me as a woman the right to vote according to my conscience, my values, and my morals.

Voting is a right that millions of Americans take for granted every election cycle. To this day, half the population doesn't participate in the vote. Why not?

**Why Don't We Vote?**

1. Many people lack an appreciation of the power of the vote. They need to understand, from an early age, the importance of voting. In the United States, voting is a privilege and a right. It's a responsibility and stewardship for the citizens. Voting needs to be held in high regard, first in the family and then in

the schools. Parents can teach their children at a young age that regardless of the outcome, voting is an obligation that must be done in the same way we pay our taxes.

2. Voting is hard because the issues that we are called upon to vote on are often complex. It takes time to study the issues and understand what the candidates believe and stand for.

3. People don't care about things that don't affect them personally. If a person doesn't own a home or a business, the tax laws don't concern them. Yet hundreds of decisions are made every day in state capitols that affect a person's life in diverse ways.

4. Voting doesn't seem to make a difference, so many people are indifferent. But in reality, voting does make a difference. Recently, here in Washington state, a House seat was overturned by the opposite party, giving them control of the House by a single seat margin. In some elections, a seat is won or lost by a single vote. When power shifts to another party, the leadership of every committee changes to the new party. This means that every bill that the leading party wants to pass will be considered first because the majority rules. This also means that the many bills by the minority party will not be considered. Bills eventually become laws, and once a law is enacted, it is difficult to reverse. So a single vote can have an impact for years.

## What Does Our Vote Represent and Where Is It Counted?

1. The President and Vice President, governors and lieutenant governors.

2. The Congress and the Senate to represent our state in Washington, D.C.

3. The state representative and state senator to represent and work on behalf of our local districts.

4. The school boards.

5. City council members.
6. County council members.
7. Tax bills.
8. Laws concerning drugs and health care—for instance, the legalization of marijuana.
9. Social laws involving marriage, parental rights, and children's rights.

When an issue is able to make it to a ballot, the voter decides which way it will go. In some instances, less than half of registered voters participate in their local elections. In the state of Washington, only 27 percent voted in the fall of 2017. That's twenty-seven out of one hundred voters.

The way to resolve this problem is by messaging. First, make sure your family and friends are registered to vote. If they are not, begin the conversation as to the important role they can assume once they become a voter. If you are a parent, don't just tell, but show. Take your children with you to the ballot box. Teach them respect for the process. Young children can learn through picture books and older children can be taught basic fundamentals of an issue (explain it in simple terms). We don't need a degree in political science to vote. There are many groups that have voter guides that can answer questions about a certain candidate or issue that is on the ballot. The media has changed. Now a person can turn to social media outlets and find out both sides of an issue on the ballot and decide which best fits their values.

Voting gives the Church and other groups an opportunity to voice their concerns and fears. Voting is the power that creates change. It's the way that Christians can participate in government.

# 18

# Election Fragility

NOVEMBER 3RD, 2020, WAS ELECTION DAY. A day forever etched in my mind. I watched a commercial for a dating website. It showed Satan trying hard to find that perfect match. Then a young woman appeared on his app; her name was 2020. The commercial was comical, showing Satan and 2020 dating and doing fun things together. At the end of the commercial, they're sitting on a park bench, looking out at the sun setting. Satan puts his arm around 2020 and says, "I just don't want this year to end."

On November 3rd, my thoughts and feelings were the exact opposite. I agreed with that commercial that 2020 was a year sent from hell, and I couldn't wait for it to end. As I watched the campaigns between President Trump and Candidate Biden, I thought there was no way that Biden would win. He couldn't even finish sentences. He and his running mate drew fewer than hundreds of people wherever they went, and they barely went anywhere to campaign.

Half of our nation went slightly into shock, watching how the votes were manipulated right before our eyes. How could this happen? There were so many irregularities in many races. The numbers were all turned upside down. For instance, let's look at the counties. Obama had 69 million votes and 873 counties. Biden has 81 million votes and 477 counties. Trump had 74 million votes and 2,497 counties. It didn't add up.

In some states, voter fraud has been going on for decades. If we have elections with integrity and fairness, three things must be dealt with immediately in our states to prevent election fraud:

1. Voter ID
2. Ballot Harvesting
3. Mail-in Voting

## 1. Voter ID

Support:

Hans von Spakovsky, The Heritage Foundation (2011):

See our page, Arguments for and against restricting who may return mail ballots, for detailed support and opposition arguments from various sources.

Those states [that have implemented voter ID laws] understand that the United States has an unfortunate history of voter fraud and that requiring individuals to authenticate their identity at the polls is a fundamental and necessary component of ensuring the integrity of the election process. Every individual who is eligible to vote should have the opportunity to do so. It is equally important, however, that the votes of eligible voters are not stolen or diluted by a fraudulent or bogus ballot cast by an ineligible or imaginary voter. The evidence from academic studies and actual turnout in elections is also overwhelming that—contrary to the shrill claims of opponents—voter ID does not depress the turnout of voters, including minority, poor, and elderly voters.

Oppose:

American Civil Liberties Union (2017):

"Voter ID laws deprive many voters of their right to vote, reduce participation, and stand in direct opposition to our country's trend of including more Americans in the democratic process. Many Americans do not have one of the forms of identification states acceptable for voting. These voters are disproportionately low-income, racial and ethnic minorities, the elderly, and people with disabilities. Such voters more frequently have difficulty obtaining ID because they cannot afford or cannot obtain the underlying documents that are a prerequisite to obtaining a government-issued photo ID card."

## 2. Ballot Harvesting.

Support:
Darrell Hill, ACLU of Arizona:

> An Arizona law stating that only family members, caregivers, and household members may return someone's ballot] burdens communities that have traditionally relied on ballot collection, such as the elderly, differently-abled, Native American, and Latino communities, by preventing them from casting a ballot in the manner that is easiest for them.

Oppose:
Hans von Spakovsky, The Heritage Foundation

> Giving third parties who have a stake in the outcome of the election access to voters and their absentee ballots in an unsupervised setting is not wise. It is a proven threat to the integrity of the election process. The handling of absentee ballots should be restricted to voters, most immediate family members, or an individual residing in their households.

## 3. Mail-in Voting

What is mail-in voting?
A: Some people distinguish between absentee and mail-in voting, while others interchange the terms. Each state has its own rules and terminology. Probably the most significant distinction is whether the state automatically mails a ballot to every registered voter or if each voter must request an absentee ballot if the voter wants to use that option.

Five states—Colorado, Hawaii, Oregon, Washington, and Utah—routinely hold by-mail elections primarily, typically with options for in-person voting and ballot drop-off sites. In response to the pandemic, at least four states—California, New Jersey, Nevada, and Vermont, plus the District of Columbia—switched to proactively mailing a ballot to every properly registered voter for the November election

Here are the arguments for Mail-in voting:

Support:

Absentee/mail-in voting reduces the spread of COVID-19.

Absentee/mail-in voting expansion is necessary to facilitate access to voting.

In-person voting forces people to choose between voting and safety.

Turnout will be low without expanded absentee/mail-in voting.

Fraud using absentee/mail-in voting is rare.

Oppose:

Absentee/mail-in voting systems can fail.

Mailed ballots go uncounted and are rejected at a higher rate.

U.S. Postal Service is unprepared for the expansion of mail voting.

Many jurisdictions are unprepared to switch to mail voting.

Absentee/mail-in voting can result in delayed election results.

Absentee/mail-in voting poses a higher risk for fraud and manipulation.

Absentee/mail-in voting provides opportunities for fraud and intimidation.

Expanding absentee/mail-in voting systems opens the door to flawed election policies. [44]

You can do further reading on all these arguments here:

https://ballotpedia.org/All-mail_voting#Debate

Congress wanted to pass a bill called H.R.1. If passed, the following items would become law:

- Universal national mail-in balloting
- Registration of 16-and 17-year-olds
- Permanent early voting
- Extended mail-in ballot acceptance past Election Day
- Minimal verification for online registration
- Legalization of ballot harvesting

- Federal matching funds to candidates for private contributions. Meaning they could launder corporate dollars through the U.S. Treasury and use those dollars to fund congressional campaigns publicly
- Voting rights for felons upon completion of their sentences

For more research and knowledge of what occurred during the 20/20 election. There are several issues covered on this website:

https://got-freedom.org/evidence/

The 2020 election brought awareness to the scope and size of voter fraud. For our elections to be as just and fair as possible, elections need to go back to in-person voting with proper identification. ID is required for everything in society today. Paper ballots are the safest way to vote, avoiding the temptation of manipulating a machine or corrupting the vote through the internet. There needs to be same-day voting with observers from both sides of the aisle observing all the ballots. Election day needs to end on election night. No more election days and weeks to give people who commit election fraud time to gather fake votes. The voting system needs a thorough cleansing to ensure the people's votes are honored and accounted fairly.

# 19

# Citizen Lobbyist

ON NOVEMBER 12, 1997, IN SCHENECTADY, NEW YORK, an eighteen-month-old tabby cat named Buster was outside doing what curious cats do—running, hiding, playing with other cats, and wondering when he'd get to eat again. On this particular night, a sixteen-year-old boy named Chester Williamson observed Buster, grabbed him, doused kerosene all over his body, and lit Buster on fire with a cigarette. Buster was found by a neighbor under a car and immediately rushed to the vet. He was so badly burned, he had to be identified by his large nose and number of toes. Buster lingered for three weeks but finally succumbed to his injuries. This led to a new law called Buster's Law. In 1999, Governor Pataki signed Buster's Law, also called the Felony Cruelty to Animals Law.[45]

In the case of Buster's Law, Nancy Bonesteel took her shocking experience of what happened to her cat and made a difference in the laws concerning animal cruelty. Buster's Law brought attention to another aspect of animal cruelty. Aside from the injuries to the pets themselves, there is evidence that violence against animals can be a precursor to violence against humans. Activists need look no further than Buster's tormentor, Williamson, to support their argument. In 2003 and 2005, Williamson was sent to prison on stolen property and burglary convictions, sentenced to up to three years in both cases. Then, on Sept. 28, 2007, just a few blocks from where he attacked Buster, Williamson, then 26, lured a 15-year-old into Vale Cemetery under the pretext of looking for her sister and attempted to rape her. Officers searching the cemetery came upon Williamson and the girl, breaking up the attack. Williamson is now serving in the state prison.[46]

**What is a Citizen Lobbyist?**

A citizen lobbyist is a person who tries to get legislators to introduce or vote for measures favorable and against measures unfavorable to an interest that he or she represents. What drives citizens to become lobbyists? Usually, it is passion for an issue that resonates with their personal or professional lives. This passion often comes because of traumatic personal experiences or deeply held beliefs about justice and personal freedoms.

In the last twenty years, tragedy has met several parents, and some of them have used what happened to their children to start foundations and change laws. In September 2006, 19-year-old Brodie Panlock ended her life after enduring ongoing humiliating and intimidating bullying by her co-workers at a café in Hawthorn, Victoria, Australia. Brodie was insulted and ridiculed, teased about her looks, held down while fish sauce was poured over her, teased about a failed suicide attempt, and had rat poison put in her bag while being taunted about being unable to kill herself. They regularly insulted her by calling her fat, stupid, ugly, and a whore. The tragedy of Brodie's death was compounded by the fact that none of those responsible for bullying Brodie were charged with a serious criminal offense under the Crimes Act 1958. Instead, each offender was convicted and fined under provisions of the Occupational Health and Safety Act. Brodie's death was a tragic reminder of the serious consequences that bullying can have on victims, their families and the community and illustrated that there were obvious limitations in the law and conduct involving serious bullying and should be subject to criminal sanctions. Because of public outrage and aggressive citizen lobbying, Brodie's Law commenced in June 2011 and made serious bullying a crime punishable by up to 10 years in jail.

In the United States, there have been other laws enacted named after victims. Megan's Law is named after seven-year-old Megan Kanka, who was raped and killed by a known child molester who had moved across the street from the family without their knowledge. In the wake of that tragedy, the Kankas' sought to have local communities warned about sex offenders in the area. All states in the U.S. now have some form of Megan's Law.

Passion for an issue doesn't need to stem from adversity. There are thousands of issues that concerned citizens can work on to make a change. The first question to ask is, "What issue brings out an emotional response when there is a discussion or debate?" Anger and fear are good indicators, and channeling those emotions through advocacy is productive. The first step in advocating and lobbying for an issue is thorough in-depth knowledge of the topic. If all a person knows about a topic is some strange headline from social media, how can that person answer in-depth questions on the topic? Studying all aspects of the topic is important to becoming an effective advocate. With every legislative issue, there are people who are for it and against it. It is important to know these things:

Who is in leadership on both sides of the issue?

Why are some for advancing the issue and why are some against advancing the issue?

What are the history and current status of the legislation concerning the issue?

What are the barriers to passing the legislation?

Simply screaming, "Our rights are being taken away, and this county is going to hell," is not going to advance a cause with the people who have the authority to change the situation.

After fully understanding the issue and preparing for every possible question, there are several ways to bring attention to the topic. One productive way is to start a petition. According to Care2petitions,

A petition, put simply, is a list of names and signatures compiled together to show support for a cause. By demonstrating public support, petitions give clout to an issue that could otherwise go overlooked by government or business. Whether you are looking to change a law or a behavior—or just raise awareness for an issue—petitions are an easy and inexpensive way to get the word out.[47]

Here are some questions to ask:
- Is your case petition ready?
- What do you need to know to make your petition ready?
- Which groups, businesses, and influencers support your cause?
- Do you have a clear target?
- Can this petition open a dialogue?[48]

One person can do a variety of things, but there is strength in numbers. That is why it's a great idea to consider joining a nonprofit organization that has similar values as your own on issues and laws that need to be implemented or changed. Partnering with an organized group helps in several ways. The most obvious one is finances. In most cases, it takes money to get attention. That is why nonprofits are getting more proficient at marketing and promoting their cause. Many organizations offer educational tools, workshops, training sessions, and conferences on fundraising. Partnering with organizations keeps the momentum and personal passion going while encouraging people to work together on the same issue, building deep and lasting friendships.

Social media is a powerful tool, but it can also be destructive if used poorly. Participating in a group discussion with comments is helpful.

Here are some important keys to remember when posting on social media:

Stay on topic with the issue that is being discussed.

Be polite, but firm. No personal insults, profanity, or name-calling.

Use social media in moderation, especially when it comes to political issues.

Hammering out tweets hourly and spouting out all day on Facebook about a topic will drive people away simply because they will tire of hearing the same thing. Updates and information are good; obsessive complaining and murmuring is not good. Negativity is never conducive to winning over your peers. It's also a good idea to create dedicated Facebook pages and other social media accounts for each topic at hand.

This way, you will be able to post on your specific topic to a targeted audience and avoid annoying your friends and family.

The most vital participation a citizen lobbyist can make is to contact their elected officials at every level of government. Although some people may feel intimidated about doing so, we should understand that our public officials work for the citizens. Still, there is a protocol for such contact. Most important is to not waste the official's time. That is why you should know the topic from beginning to end and be specific about what you want the official to do. Next, make sure you are reaching the right person. Is your issue a city, state, or federal issue? It could be a combination, so educate yourself in order to communicate with the right people. Find out who are your state and U.S. legislators. It's easy to check. Just log on to your state government website, type in your zip code, and in most states, the website will direct you right to the correct legislator in your district.

Investigation is easier these days because every branch of government has a website. For instance, here in Washington State, the website is leg.wa.gov. From there, a person can get information on bills, committees, scheduled hearings, and floor sessions. There are separate pages within the website specifically for the House and Senate Republicans and Democrats. Further, each legislator has a personal page, and that page shows what bills they are sponsoring. When the state legislature is in session, there will be 4,000 to 5,000 bills for them to consider. It's simply impossible for them to understand every issue. In many instances, they are instructed by their caucus on how to vote.

In order to be an effective citizen lobbyist, a person has to think from the perspective of a legislator. According to the Family Policy Institute of Washington State, "To influence the behavior of a legislator, there needs to be knowledge of what motivates their decisions." [49]

Fundamentally, there are three types of legislators. The first is the legislator that agrees with the issue and is participating on the same team. The second legislator is equally against the issue and on the opposite side. Then there is the third legislator that sits squarely in the middle. It is this third legislator that determines what issues get voted on and is the deciding vote on controversial bills. He or she is the person who needs to be persuaded on the issues.

There are four distinct ways to educate a legislator:

1. Facts
2. Studies
3. Budgets
4. Policy arguments

When approaching a legislator, it is important to understand their thinking and motivation on key issues. The number one deciding factor with many votes is, "How will it impact their reelection?" The next question is, "Do they have a conviction about the issue?" If they do— one way or another—it will be difficult to make a persuasive argument. If there is no conviction about the issue, the legislator will consider your arguments.

Now, to a legislator, thinking about an issue is not the same thought process as a vote. A voter looks at an issue from deeply held values. A legislator—especially those in the middle—will ponder several things before casting a vote:

### Interest Groups

Will the vote affect the interest groups that are giving them money? Chairmanships

Will the vote jeopardize future leadership positions within the party?

### Peer Groups

What kind of consequences will come from peers and associations? Impact on position in caucus

Will the vote upset the party line and caucus?

### Higher Office

Will the vote impact future chances for higher office?

A citizen lobbyist needs to identify and get to know the legislators who can be persuaded—those in the middle. Build a respectful relationship with your legislator, not a combative one. The middle legislator needs to become an ally. Work on discovering their focus and goals for their term. Getting involved with issues that are bipartisan is a good head start in relationship building. The goal is to build bridges, not burn them.

Here are three ways to reach out to legislators.

**1. Phone calls**

Every legislator has a phone number listed on the state capitol website. Their phone will usually be answered by their legislative assistant or staffer. Still, these are human beings, so don't be a robot reading off a template. Their offices get those types of phone calls every day, so droning on and on will do little to advance your cause. Instead, explain in your own words your opinions and feelings about the issue. Stay on topic and to the point. Two good times to call are at the beginning of the legislative session and right before the vote.

**2. Email**

Every legislator has an email that can be taken directly from the State Capitol website. Be specific with emails. When addressing a government official, in person or in print, use the proper salutation. This signals to your representative or senator that you respect their position, and they will be more likely to take you seriously.

The proper salutation for a U.S. senator is "Dear Senator <name>."

The proper salutation for a U.S. representative is "Dear Mr./Mrs./Ms. <name>."

Of course, there is no legal requirement to use a particular salutation. You're free to call your senator or representative whatever you like. However, you will gain favor and be taken more seriously if you respect the office of the person you're contacting.

It is also important to write with a friendly yet professional tone. Your email doesn't have to be a work of art but it needs to be free of spelling and grammar mistakes. Access the plethora of editorial software available; much of it is free (such as Grammarly). Finally, if you're asking the official for a particular change, be firm and state your position clearly.

You may include personal details but try to keep them relevant to the topic at hand.

Keep written correspondence short. Don't write more than a few paragraphs if you want your reader to stay with you. Make sure you say what you need to say. Condense any anecdotes as much as possible.

Try to keep it under 500 words, and be polite and courteous.

### 3. Visit in person

Visiting your legislators can be daunting, but most of them realize they work for their constituents, and so they will listen to your concerns. Make an appointment in advance. Prepare for your meeting with a written outline. Greet them with grace, especially if they are from the other side of the aisle. Find some issue they have voted on or sponsored where there is an agreement between both of you and thank them for it. Be courteous, smile, and get to the topic. If you are nervous, you might forget an important point, so bring a note card and keep it close. Stay away from generalities such as, "We need better education!" or, "The roads are a mess." Bring the issue to your personal experience. How will the issue affect you, your family, and your community? Explain in detail the consequences and the benefits of their vote. The legislators need to be reminded that their votes affect thousands of people exactly like the one sitting across from them.

And again, do not waste their time. Choose your words carefully, and give them time to process your information. They are busy people; respect that.

In conclusion, be alert and stay abreast of the information affecting your issue. Join groups, use social media, sign petitions, march at rallies, and visit your legislator face to face. You can make a huge impact for today and change your world for tomorrow.

# 20

# <u>The Neighborhood</u>

IT WAS 6:00 P.M. AND AMY WAS ON HER EVENING RUN when a neighbor that she never met rushed up to her and said, "Amy? Are you Amy? Please get in the car. There's an issue with your son." Without hesitation, she jumped in the car and allowed the man to drive her to her home. Upon arrival, there were police cars and an ambulance parked at her home.

"Is my son okay?" she cried out. "What happened? Where are our other boys?"

Here is the rest of the story in her words.

> After his third "I don't know…your husband just asked me to find you" response, I tried to silence my chatter. When we finally pulled up to our house, I saw my husband, Brandon, on his knees, head on the grass, with a small, shirtless body lying next to him: my Jack.
>
> "Is he gone?" I squeaked, inching my way in beside Jack amidst a sea of unfamiliar faces. My heart was in my throat, and I was shaking.
>
> Brandon lifted his head and brought his hands to his face. He couldn't speak. He looked ghost-white. Horrified. Broken. A stranger, a petite blond with warm eyes and a calming demeanor, stepped up to me. "I didn't think I could save him," she said, "but I did CPR, and I think he's okay."
>
> I later learned that her name was Barbie. She was a registered nurse, and though I'd never seen her before, she lived across the street from us.

Her words hung in the air.

*Didn't think she could save him? He had actually been gone? Not breathing? She had brought him back to life?*

I reached for her hand and squeezed it, then scooped Jack into my arms and collapsed on the grass, speechless with the terror of what might have been.

What could I say to the woman who had literally saved my son's life, the woman who hadn't thought she could save my baby but had tried—and done it? Her will, her skill, and her breath had brought him back to us.[50] This is one story among countless others of how the people living right next to us have the potential to help in times of crisis. Think about it. Our neighbors share our most intimate space, our everyday natural life. What are those spaces? They are our homes, roads, shopping malls, restaurants, schools—everything a person needs to live life is shared with our neighbors. Yet according to Brian Bethune in his article "The End of Neighbors", "More than 30 percent of Canadians now say they feel disconnected from their neighbors, while half of Americans admit they don't know the names of theirs, and a recent poll of 2000 Britons found a third couldn't pick out their neighbors out of a police lineup."[51]

It's worse than not knowing our neighbors, however. In recent times, we have stopped caring for our neighbors. Yes, social media has brought a social revolution, but neighborhood involvement has been declining for decades. Neighbors stopped talking to each other long before video games and Facebook. One reason for this is economics. Fifty years ago, families lived on one spouse's income while the other spouse—usually the mother—stayed at home. This brought a neighborhood filled with family members watching over each other's children and properties. Now, most neighborhoods are completely vacant during the day with a few hours in the later afternoon and evening occupied by latchkey kids playing video games, watching TV, or on social media. Compounding the problem is the fact that when we are home, we are usually recovering from the day, and by then it's difficult to get out of our personal space and reach out to a stranger, even when that stranger lives one hundred feet from your front door or shares a backyard fence.

The tragedy in this social evolution is that the neighborhood remains the most available evangelistic field for most Christians. Most of us will not be able to go to Africa, but we can reach out to the single mom or the lonely elderly man across the street, as scarce as they are becoming. According to Scripture, Christians are to love their neighbor as themselves. In Luke 10, the question posed to Jesus was, "Who is my neighbor?" His answer became the parable of the good Samaritan.

In reply Jesus said:

> *"A man was going down from Jerusalem to Jericho, when he was attacked by robbers. They stripped him of his clothes, beat him, and went away, leaving him half dead. A priest happened to be going down the same road, and when he saw the man, he passed by on the other side. So too, a Levite, when he came to the place and saw him, passed by on the other side. But a Samaritan, as he traveled, came where the man was; and when he saw him, he took pity on him. He went to him and bandaged his wounds, pouring on oil and wine. Then he put the man on his own donkey, brought him to an inn, and took care of him. The next day he took out two denarii and gave them to the innkeeper. 'Look after him,' he said, 'and when I return, I will reimburse you for any extra expense you may have.'*
>
> *"Which of these three do you think was a neighbor to the man who fell into the hands of robbers?"*
>
> *The expert in the law replied, "The one who had mercy on him."*
>
> *Jesus told him, "Go and do likewise."*

Luke 10:30-37

According to the teaching of Christ, this word "neighbor" is any other man irrespective of race or religion with whom we live or whom we chance to meet (which idea is clearly brought out in the parable).[52]

Jesus used this parable to dig out from the Jewish community an ugly root of racism, but he also dealt with people's tendencies to look the other way and refused to get involved. This parable teaches us just the opposite. When a need becomes evident, the Christian community is expected to fill that need and not ignore it.

> *What good is it, my brothers and sisters, if someone claims to have faith but has no deeds? Can such faith save them? Suppose a brother or a sister is without clothes and daily food. If one of you says to them, "Go in peace; keep warm and well fed," but does nothing about their physical needs, what good is it? In the same way, faith by itself, if it is not accompanied by action, is dead.*

James 2:14-17

How does the Church participate in government by being a good neighbor? Well, the neighborhood consists of homeowners and taxpayers, and each group has certain rights and authority. As such, a neighborhood is a form of government. Taking responsibility to bless and help the neighborhood is releasing God's light in the darkness.

Indeed, there here are many ways to engage people in the local neighborhood. It's important to build relationships in the neighborhood so that when there is a crisis, the neighbors will know whom they can ask for help, prayer, or guidance. In most instances, personal salvation comes first from the seed, then the shoot, then the final harvest. The ideas below are ways to start planting seeds and sharing the love of God.

Here are some great ideas:
- Get to know your neighbors. If you can't name more than a neighbor or two, it's time to introduce yourself. Even if you've lived in your home for a while, this first introduction

doesn't need to be awkward or a big production. Simply smile and say, "Hey, I've been meaning to introduce myself…"

- Hang out on your porch or in your front yard. It's hard to get to know your neighbors if you don't ever see them. Just by being out in front of your house, you can give off a welcoming vibe that encourages interaction. If I am out in front, especially with the kids, every neighbor who walks by, even those I don't know, still smiles and says hello. Create a block directory. If you don't yet know your neighbors, this is the perfect way to get started. It doesn't need to be fancy. Just drop off a sign-up sheet in everyone's mailbox, and, once they return it to you, you can email the final version to everyone.
- Be respectful of your neighbors. Don't be that guy they all talk about. Clean up after your dog, and keep it leashed when out walking. Be aware of any disturbing noise levels that you are creating. Maintain your property, and respect property boundaries.
- Organize a block party. I didn't learn most of my neighbors' names until we had our first block party. After that one party, it seemed there was a lot more interaction on our block. This idea does involve a little work, but if you share the coordinating duties with other neighbors and keep it simple (at least that first year), this is an easy way to get to know your neighbors.
- Build a little free library. As a book lover and a community builder, I've always loved the idea of the little free library. And we're lucky to have two within a couple of blocks of our house (one a residence, one a business). Each little free library is registered online, so you can even see if there already is one near you.
- Build a community garden. This is a time-tested way to promote community interaction in your neighborhood as well

as share in a bounty of fresh veggies. Check out the American Community Gardening Association's steps for getting started.

- Host a backyard movie night. Treat the neighborhood to your favorite movie.

- Create a formalized tool-sharing program. Sure, you can just ask Joe next door if you can borrow his drill, but consider establishing a more formal tool-sharing program to get everyone involved. I love this idea because tools are one of those things that you generally only use once in a while, so why not share them when they're not in use? Local Tools is an online lending library management system that can get you started. Or check out Peerby or Streetbank to see if your neighbors are already participating.

- Welcome new families. You can bring a traditional baked good, but I also love the idea of welcoming newcomers by sharing your favorite local restaurants and businesses, perhaps with a stack of your favorite take-out menus wrapped up in ribbon.

- Establish a neighborhood watch program. These programs can be one of the most effective deterrents to neighborhood crime. Check out the National Crime Prevention Council's guide to getting started.

- Celebrate Neighbor Day in April. Since 2010, Good Magazine has sponsored Neighbor Day on the last Saturday of April by providing tools and suggestions to encourage good neighboring. You can check the website to get neighborly inspiration from all over the globe.

- Host a regular monthly gathering, the same time, no RSVP needed. Years ago, I read in Sunset Magazine (unfortunately, the article does not appear to be archived online) about a woman who hosted a monthly soup social at her house. The idea was simple: She provided the soup, and neighbors would bring a baguette or drink to share, and their own bowl. And this was key: She held it at the same time every month and no RSVP was necessary. A regular gathering that requires no commitment and little forethought makes for an easygoing gathering.

- Start a neighborhood book club. In my last neighborhood, we had a block book club. When you only have to walk two houses over, it is a lot easier to be able to participate. Or if that feels like too much commitment (and when your kids are young, reading an entire book each month can feel like an unattainable goal), consider something slightly different, such as an "articles club."

- Shovel your neighbor's sidewalk when it snows, especially if it is difficult for them. If your neighbors are older or perhaps just going through a hard time with a new baby or sickness, spend a few extra minutes to clear their sidewalk too. This is no small gesture. In Denver, homeowners can actually be ticketed if their sidewalks aren't clear 24 hours after it snows, even if they are out of town. Plus, you never know who will return the favor.

- Support your neighborhood schools. There is a reason the most successful schools are the ones where parents are actively engaged. Good schools have successful, if informal, partnerships between the administration, the parents, and the community-at-large. Even if you don't have kids at the school, it's important to remember that the local school is also a member of the community and can greatly impact the neighborhood, positively or negatively. Our neighborhood businesses frequently host fundraisers to benefit the local schools. If you can attend an event, you're helping the school as well as getting to know your neighbors at a fun community event. Address concerns or issues directly with your neighbor. Don't let a problem fester and escalate. And don't immediately call to report a problem to the city without first trying to work it out with your neighbor directly.

- Host a porch party. This is something I've always wanted to do! I love hanging out on my front porch, and a porch party feels like an easy way to socialize with your neighbors without the work of a "real" party.

- Shop locally if you live near a business district. You will not only see and interact with your neighbors at the local businesses and along the way, but you will also get to know your other neighbors, the local business owners, and employees.

- Support our youngest entrepreneurs by buying the neighbor kids' lemonade. I once read somewhere you should always buy whatever kids are selling on card tables in their front yards. I think it goes back to the "it takes a village" concept where you're helping to encourage the initiative and resourcefulness of the young. Plus, just think back to when you were a kid and you were so excited to have a lemonade stand. You made all of the lemonade and spent an hour working on your sign, and then you sat and waited and waited. And when that first customer finally showed up, it didn't matter that you only made fifty cents; you were so excited. Be that person for the neighborhood kids.

- Treat your neighbors to a front-yard concert. Music has always been something that brings people together. Still, this one's a little tricky and depends on the neighborhood. Many would welcome a guitarist strumming on his front steps but perhaps not a full band. You have to know your neighborhood and, of course, be aware and respectful of noise levels. Check out Boulder's Mapleton PorchFest for inspiration.

- Share your skills. Are you tech-savvy? Perhaps you can sew or like to tinker with cars. Your neighbors would love for you to share these skills with them, either by teaching them or just helping on a one-time basis. Skill-sharing banks are popping up in neighborhoods across the country.

- Talk to other parents at the park. The neighborhood park is where I get the best scoop! If you have kids, the neighborhood playground can offer a wealth of info: which schools parents like and why, where the best activities for kids are, and which new restaurants are coming to the neighborhood. Exchanging neighborhood info at the park is a time-honored tradition among parents, but so often today everyone is on their smartphone. And I admit I've been that mom. But I've also learned to make play dates and gather neighborhood intel.

- Coordinate a neighborhood yard sale. Garage sale, tag sale, yard sale...whatever name you call it, this is a good way to clear out your home's clutter and help your neighbors do the same.

- Start a networking group. As the old nursery song goes, you just never know "who are the people in your neighborhood, the people who you meet each day." One of them just might be the perfect person for you to connect with professionally. Who knows? Your next position or client could be as close as the guy who lives four houses down. Meet up at a neighborhood coffee shop, and publicize it on their community board to cast a wider net in the neighborhood.

- Let your neighbors know when you will be out of town, and ask them to contact you or the police if anything is suspicious. You don't need a formalized neighborhood watch program to keep the neighborhood safe. My next-door neighbor had a break-in stopped by a helpful neighbor who knew she was traveling. If you ask your neighbors, they will likely ask you in turn, which helps to keep the neighborhood safe for everyone.

- Welcome new little ones to the neighborhood. When I was growing up, every time one of the families had a new baby, the neighbors would decorate the family's front porch with pink or blue ribbons. It was a small gesture, but a way of simultaneously announcing to everyone the baby's birth and welcoming the baby into our community.

- Share small neighborhood gifts at holiday times. It's rare that anyone gets anything fun in the mail these days. Why not surprise your neighbor with a holiday treat? Keep it simple: baked goods, seasoned popcorn, or even a bottle of wine will be welcomed by most.

- Drive like your kids live here because they do! I have become one of those people who yell, "Slow down!" whenever a car speeds down our street, which means I've become my parents. But I get it now that I have kids. We all like to live in vibrant, bustling neighborhoods, but this means people, especially kids, need to feel safe when walking or biking around.

- Connect online to connect offline. Websites like Next Door have created whole new online neighborhoods, but it's important to remember to not use these sites in place of actually getting to know our neighbors in real life. So, go ahead and create that neighborhood Facebook group page. But, be sure to use it to encourage offline interaction, too.[53]

# 21

# City Government

## *September 11, 2001*

THE ATTACK ON THE TWIN TOWERS IN NEW YORK CITY was an attack of unprecedented magnitude. This quote by then-mayor Rudy Giuliani captures the feeling well.

> And as we are walking toward the scene, which was only two blocks away, looking up, all of a sudden I see a man throwing himself out of the 101st, 102nd floor. And I would say that experience, I describe it as like a switch. It just changed all my emotions. I went from sort of a feeling that I'm walking through an emergency that I can handle, that we've had before. We have a game plan. We know everybody has their role. When I saw that, I just exclaimed to people around me, "This is much worse than anything we've ever faced before. It's off the charts. We're just going to have to make up our response, we don't have a plan for this."

> And that scene, of the man throwing himself off the building, I probably relive more than any other. When I go back to September 11th and think about it-lots of memories, but the one persistent and most difficult one is watching that man throw himself from the 101st, 102nd floor. Because it probably shocked me, and I just watched the whole thing. I just stopped and watched the whole thing.[54]

With the president out of sight for most of that day, Giuliani became the voice of America. Every time he spoke, millions of people felt a little better. His words were full of grief and iron, inspiring New York to inspire the nation.

> Tomorrow New York is going to be here. And we're going to rebuild, and we're going to be stronger than we were before…I want the people of New York to be an example to the rest of the country, and the rest of the world, that terrorism can't stop us.[55]

New York City is the largest city in the United States. Being the mayor of that city is a weighty position with massive accountability. But on September 11, even the mayor had no idea what it would entail to be a civil servant. A huge need appeared that day, requiring him to become more than a mayor. He became a light and a hero for millions.

In the city of Seattle, there is a plan to build heroin injection sites for addicts. In response, Jon Nehring, the mayor of Marysville, Washington, (a community north of Seattle), and his son Nate Nehring (who has a seat in the Snohomish County council) brought concerns to the county council regarding injection sites in their community. The Snohomish County Council unanimously voted against having heroin injection sites brought into their region. Not only did they ban injection sites, but the local government is currently taking proactive steps to prevent an infestation of homeless addicts. They are launching the new North County Law Enforcement-Embedded Social Worker Team, as well as a new county chronic nuisance ordinance. There will be two social workers from the county and three law enforcement officers going into encampments where the homeless and drug-addicted dwell. The goal is to offer assistance and connect them with treatment, job training, and services that will sustain them until they are fully capable of living a healthy and stable life. If they refuse, under the new law, the lifestyle of an addict will not be tolerated. Many of these addicts commit property crimes and abuse the local community. If the addict does not want to change, they will be removed from the city. This is tough love, yet in this case, the local government is taking responsibility for their community. (As a side note, both Jon Nehring and his son, Nate, are Christians.)

Getting involved in local city government may not always be that dramatic, but people in every city need strong leaders and visionaries to help guide and build the city. Cities need leaders who have integrity, leaders who are fearless and bold in decision making, and leaders who are full of faith. Cities need leaders who will protect and oversee the citizens with care. And yet, at a deeper level, Scripture says this about Christians who live in cities.

> *When the righteous prosper, the city rejoices; when the wicked perish, there are shouts of joy. Through the blessing of the upright a city is exalted, but by the mouth of the wicked it is destroyed.*

> Proverbs 11:10-11

Christian leadership is vital to any city.

> *Unless the Lord watches over the city, the guards stand watch in vain.*

> Psalm 127:1

How does the Lord watch over the city? He watches over the city through his servants, including his civil servants. And to what end? Well, at the end of the age, there will be a separation of sheep and goat nations. Is it possible there could be the same for cities? Cities are a creation of God, so much so that at the end of the age, the glorious bride comes down as a beautiful city. These earthy cities could be training for ruling and leading in the ages to come. Christian men and women could completely transform their cities from corruption and poverty by faith in God and by the wisdom of the Holy Spirit.

The local city government has several departments and many services, all necessary to keep a city functioning at peak performance. In fact, it's breathtaking to take in how a local city works.

Here is a basic list of city departments and a definition of a few of their roles:

**Mayor**

The mayor occupies the highest elective office in the municipal government and is expected to provide the leadership necessary to keep the city moving in the proper direction. Effective mayors see themselves not only as leaders staking out policy positions but also as facilitators of effective teamwork.

As a mayor, you have a special set of long-term responsibilities not shared by many others. You are supposed to be a community leader and a political leader. Yet most of the trials and tribulations you will face during your term of office will deal with city housekeeping. These day-to-day activities are of immediate concern to most residents, and sometimes solving the little problems is the most fun.

Ceremonial role: The mayor's participation in local ceremonial events is a never-ending responsibility. On a daily basis, the mayor is expected to cut ribbons at ceremonies to open new businesses, break ground for the construction of new city facilities, and regularly appear at fairs, parades, and other community celebrations. The mayor also issues proclamations for a variety of purposes. As a featured speaker before professional clubs, school assemblies, and neighborhood groups, the mayor can expect to be interviewed, photographed, and otherwise placed on extensive public display by the media.

Intergovernmental relations: The city does not operate in a vacuum. Cities must work within a complex intergovernmental system. City officials keep in contact and cooperate with your federal, state, county, and school officials. Mayors take the lead in representing their local government to those from outside the community who are interested in joint ventures-including other local governments, regional organizations, and federal and state government representatives. In this area, mayors promote a favorable image of their local government and pursue resources that will benefit the community.

Public relations: Mayors inform the public, the media, and staff about issues affecting the community. This role is critical in building public support and facilitating effective decision-making by the council.

Working with residents: Mayors listen to complainants, inform the residents, and encourage participation.

**The City Council**

In general, it is the council's role to adopt policies for the city and it is the mayor's role to administer or carry out those policies. The council, being legislative, has the power to enact laws and policies, consistent with state law, usually through the enactment of ordinances and resolutions. The council also has specific authority to:

- Enact a city budget.
- Define the powers, functions, and duties of city officers and employees.
- Fix the compensation of officers and employees.
- Establish the working conditions of officers and employees.
- Maintain retirement and pension systems.
- Impose fines and penalties for violation of city ordinances.
- Enter into contracts.
- Regulate the acquisition, sale, ownership, and other disposition of real property.
- Provide governmental, recreational, educational, cultural, and social services.
- Impose taxes, if not prohibited by state law.
- Cause the city to own and operate utilities.
- Approve claims against the city.
- Grant franchises for the use of public ways.
- License, for the purpose of revenue and regulation, most any type of business.

In addition, the council is authorized to enact rules governing its procedures, including for public meetings and hearings.[56]

### Police Department

Police officers are trained and sworn to uphold law and order. A normal duty shift might include transporting a drunk driver to a detoxification facility, intervening in a domestic assault, citing underage drinkers, apprehending a shoplifter, handling a traffic accident, investigating burglaries, and executing search warrants. Each call requires completion of forms and reports.

Occasionally, an officer will be summoned to testify in court about the incident and circumstances of the arrest. Along with traditional duties, police officers today engage in many proactive initiatives. They get out of their cars, walk around, and interact with families and business owners in their assigned neighborhoods. An effort is made to get acquainted on a first-name basis with leaders of schools, organizations, and churches.

Examples of proactive outreach include helping to organize a neighborhood watch, giving presentations to schools, and speaking to residents about their concerns at a neighborhood association meeting. Building trust with diverse communities and working collaboratively to address social issues, such as gang violence, is an especially important function of the police.[57]

The Bible has some interesting Scriptures about police officers, besides the duties already listed. Romans 12:4 says,

> *For the one in authority is God's servant for your good. But if you do wrong, be afraid, for rulers do not bear the sword for no reason. They are God's servants, agents of wrath to bring punishment on the wrongdoer.*

One translation calls rulers policemen. Notice what the Lord calls these rulers with swords: his *servants*. They are his servants for our good. How much better if these servants were the bearers of Christ's light?

Here are some other departments and their roles taken from the City of Marysville, Washington website:

### Fire Department

Besides putting out fires, the fire department educates the public about these workshops and services:

- Smoke alarms and carbon dioxide detectors
- Preventing falls for older adults
- Blood pressure checks
- Child passenger safety
- Bike helmet program
- Address signs
- CPR classes

### Courts

Court judges have jurisdiction to preside over traffic infractions, misdemeanors, gross misdemeanors, and codes.

### Community Development

Community development is a one-stop shop for developers, citizens, and property owners to obtain information, permits, online payment of residential permits, and assistance on all aspects of land use and land development. It enhances customer service by providing easy access to staff and planning and building documents while streamlining the permit process. It provides consistency and predictability of land development from the initial planning stages all the way to final approval.

### Finance

The finance department provides financial services for the city. It provides staff and citizens with services in accounting, taxes, treasury, budgeting, capital investment, purchasing, and contracting.

### Parks and Recreation

The parks, culture, and recreation department's focus is to enhance the quality of life by providing beautiful parks, open spaces, and exceptional recreational and athletic programs. The department has a long history of providing the public with exceptional parks and services for children, families, and individuals by providing a safe and fun environment for everyone to experience.

The parks, culture and recreation department coordinate several festivals and events each year. A wide variety of recreation and athletics classes, camps, leagues, trips, and tours are available year-round to cater to the active and creative spirit in everyone.

**Public Works**

From traffic signals to wastewater treatment plants, the public works department provides leadership in preparing, building, and maintaining the infrastructure that provides for our community's needs today and for the generations of tomorrow.

Regular operations include:

- Maintaining and constructing sewer, water lines, and storm drain systems
- Maintaining water quality
- Managing surface water
- Maintaining the wastewater treatment plant
- Maintaining traffic signals and street signs
- Striping, sweeping, and maintaining streets for all weather conditions
- Managing engineering/capital projects
- Maintaining the solid waste, recycling, and yard debris program
- Providing mapping services
- Maintaining city vehicles and facilities
- Purchasing and distributing supplies for department operations
- Providing administrative support for the department as well as customer service

The people who work for the city are called public servants for a good reason. For the most part, public servants will not become rich from their position. Unlike the corrupt early years, city officials have a passion and love for their city. The first thing a person can do to get involved in city government is to attend a local city council meeting, ask questions and get to know the leaders of the community. In a city, a person can touch others in a variety of ways. The easiest way a person can participate in city government is by shopping and purchasing locally. The city sales tax goes into the city coffers. Invest where you live. It's a great first start.

# 22

# The Schools

CHILDREN WILL SPEND HALF OF THEIR LIVES IN SCHOOL starting around the age of six and ending around the age of twenty-one. Where a child lives and how much money the family makes will determine the quality of instruction he or she will receive. Parents have options, but those options revolve around finances and time. There are several ways a child can be educated. The local public school, a private institution, charter schools, homeschooling, and tutoring. Most families place their children in public schools. Public school requires very little parental involvement other than the child bringing home notices and parent/teacher conferences. In some instances, the public school teaches things that are contrary to the parents' values and religious beliefs. In these cases, the parents have rightful authority to challenge the school.

Here are some examples where public schools have crossed the line.

Mackenzie Frazier, a sixth-grader at Somerset Academy, a public charter school in Las Vegas, Nevada, was told that she could not include a Bible verse in a class assignment titled "All About Me." An organization called First Liberty sent a demand letter to school officials informing them that the law protects the expression of faith by students in class assignments. Two days later, the school responded with a formal apology and allowed Mackenzie to resubmit her assignment including her expression of faith.

First Liberty is one of several organizations dedicated to *"defending and protecting our country's most cherished and profound freedom: religious liberty."*[58]

Here are more stories from their archives.

A teacher at Park Lakes Elementary School in Ft. Lauderdale, FL, ordered Giovanni Rubeo to stop reading his Bible during the free reading time, saying, "Put it on my desk." The teacher then left a voicemail for Giovanni's father, telling him that "those books" were not allowed in her classroom. First Liberty Institute sent a letter to the school, demanding an official apology and restoration of students' rights. The school rescinded the threats, ensuring that Giovanni and his peers may now read their Bibles during free time.

First Liberty Institute successfully protected the religious freedom rights of Audrey Jarvis, a college student at Sonoma State University in California who was told by a supervisor to remove a cross necklace while she was working at a student orientation fair. First Liberty helped Audrey file a request for religious accommodation with the university. After an investigation by the university, the school's president issued Audrey a formal apology.

Audrey's story demonstrates that religious liberty can be preserved when those who experience the violation of their rights courageously take a stand. Audrey's case made headlines across the country, bringing attention to the growing attacks on religious freedom in America's schools and universities.

Angela Hildenbrand, the valedictorian of her class and a model student at Medina Valley High School near San Antonio, Texas, planned to pray during her graduation speech. However, a federal judge banned prayer from the school's graduation ceremony and threatened incarceration for anyone who disobeyed his order. First Liberty Institute filed an emergency motion for intervention and request for relief on Angela's behalf at the U.S. Court of Appeals for the

Fifth Circuit. The Fifth Circuit overturned the lower court's ruling and protected Angela's right to pray at her graduation ceremony.

The federal district court's order violated Angela's constitutional rights to religious liberty and free speech. The government cannot censor the religious speech of its citizens, including public school students. The First Amendment of the U.S. Constitution guarantees the rights of free speech and free exercise of religion, and the U.S. Supreme Court affirmed that students do not "shed their constitutional rights to freedom of speech or expression at the schoolhouse gate" (Tinker v. Des Moines Independent Community School District, 1969).[59] Consider this line from the previous paragraph: "Students do not shed their constitutional rights to freedom of speech or expression at the schoolhouse gate." This is a profound sentence. Christians need to be thankful for the right to voice their belief in Christ. In order to keep this right strong, Christians can step up to the plate and participate in their children's school. Public schools are government-sponsored institutions funded by the taxpayer and administered by school boards and school superintendents. Once a child enters under that "public gate," they come under authority. That authority has the power to instill values and beliefs contrary to the parent or guardian over that child. Because of strong civil authority, parents and guardians are often manipulated or intimated by teachers, principals, and administrators. These gatekeepers hold great power, but they do not have the highest authority over children. Children belong to their parents, not the government. Parents need to recognize the battle in which we are engaged.

Nehemiah faced a similar battle when he undertook to build a wall and restore the gates of Jerusalem. Nehemiah 4:17-18 reads, "Those who carried burdens were loaded in such a way that each labored on the work with one hand and held his weapon with the other. And each of the builders had his sword strapped to his side while he built." Obviously, Nehemiah wasn't looking for a fight—the objective was to finish building the wall—but he recognized that he had to be prepared for battle.

Parents are engaged in building families. In so doing, they are required to engage and uplift their families, but also to defend and protect them. Good parenting means being proactive in the children's lives. It is vital that parents operate from both offensive and defensive positions when it comes to their families.

> *Teach them to your children, talking about them when you sit at home and when you walk along the road, when you lie down and when you get up.*
>
> Deuteronomy 11:19

> *Arise, cry out in the night, as the watches of the night begin; pour out your heart like water in the presence of the Lord. Lift up your hands to him for the lives of your children.*
>
> Lamentations 2:19

These Scriptures (and there are many more on this topic) are instructing parents to pray for their children and teach them the Word of God daily. This is the offensive tactic. The defensive tactic is going on the battlefield and protecting the children from the corrupt influences of our day.

In recent years, government-run schools have tried to indoctrinate children on a variety of subjects. A recent development is the attempt to remove the pronouns "he" and "she" from the English vocabulary. The argument is that calling a boy a boy and a girl a girl is somehow discriminatory. This is how far the public-school rabbit hole will go without accountability and oversight. There are 48 million students in the United States, 90 percent of whom attend public schools.

Consider the power that school boards wield:
- Taxing authority
- Employing the superintendent
- Developing and adopting policies, curriculum, and budget

- Overseeing facilities issues
- Adopting collective bargaining agreements

To get in front of the issue and to ensure the best possible outcomes for the next generation, it is vital that Christians participate in the public-school forum at a much deeper and more focused level. School board members are elected, so run for office. Becoming a school board member will keep the Christian community abreast of what types of curricula, events, and worldviews are promoted by public schools and handed down to our children.

Here are some other ways parents and guardians can participate in government-run schools.

### PTA

The Parent Teacher Association is a national organization geared toward building strong relationships between parents, teachers, and administrators. This relationship is for the sole purpose of strengthening and advocating for students.

The PTA provides the following benefits:

- Regular updates on school activities and policies
- Access to teachers and administrators at your child's school
- Access to parents of other children at the school
- A forum to discuss concerns and problems at school
- Access to resources on parenting, education, and more from the National PTA
- Appreciation from teachers for all your help
- Education about school policies, state funding, and other issues concerning your school

If the problem needs attention from the state or national government, any local, district, or state PTA can bring the issue to the attention of the national PTA.

The PTA is an extensive organization and a great place to get rooted in your local community for the children. Parents and guardians don't need a college degree to be involved and can still be strong pillars for the children and youth in their sphere of influence.

Here is an extensive list of the things the PTA does for the school districts:

Learning: PTA supports a rich, well-rounded curriculum for all students—not just reading, writing, and arithmetic, and not just textbooks, rote learning, and bubble tests. All children deserve literature, history, the arts, hands-on math and science, project-based learning, physical education, sports opportunities, and more.

The Arts: PTA supports the arts for all students. That means diving in and making things, performing, or writing. It's all about creative expression, not just observing someone else's work.

Children's Health: Many PTAs act in supporting roles to ensure children's health needs are met. Health issues impact a child's entire life, including his or her ability to focus, study, and learn. Imagine trying to absorb knowledge while suffering from a toothache.

Beginning with prenatal care and "well-baby care," parents should make sure that their children have routine medical and dental checkups so that problems are averted or discovered and treated as early as possible. Check for vision and hearing problems. It's hard to learn if you can't hear the teacher, or if you can't see the board.

Mental Health: PTAs and other organizations offer parental education, especially in areas of social/emotional health such as anxiety, depression, substance abuse, and bullying.

Parent Education: PTAs all over the country offer talks and workshops on health and safety, learning, special education, parenting, and other topics. Most are free; many are open to everyone. Did you know that the SCCOE presents over 200 free workshops each school year? Colleges and universities, hospitals and clinics, foundations, churches, and other agencies and nonprofits all over the country also offer great talks and workshops (some free).[60]

**Booster Clubs**

My parents divorced when I was ten years old. At the beginning of the divorce, my siblings and I were required to live with our father instead of our mother. My father was not a Christian and didn't understand the purpose of marriage and family, but he was a hardcore disciplinarian who loved sports. At ten years old, he signed me up for a girls' softball league in the city. That was probably the greatest accomplishment of parenting he did for me. I was a natural. I learned quickly how to play and became a champion ball player. In the process, I learned discipline and the importance of being part of a team. I learned what it felt like to win and what it felt like to lose miserably. My dad never missed a game and kept me in sports until the middle of my high school years. His directing me into sports saved me from the substance abuse and lawlessness that often comes from hours of inactivity and boredom.

Parents and guardians need to understand the importance of attending their children's events and strive to play an active role. Joining a booster club or starting one for their school sports teams can be a way to become more involved, fostering accountability with the coaches and teachers who are involved in the school team sports.

Here is a brief description of what a booster club does (according to Steele Canyon High School's club):

- Raise money to defer costs of athletics, athletic team support, and the Athletic Department of SCHS.
- Strive to improve positive communication between school coaches, the school administration, student athletes, and parents.
- Provide rewarding opportunities for parents to participate in their student's athletic experience.
- Raise money through memberships, fundraising events, merchandise sales, concession sales, corporate sponsorships, and generous donations.

- Help organize and empower Team Liaisons to make certain every team is represented and fellow parents receive necessary information. [61]

As good as children's sports programs can be, they can also inflict harm. I've met many people whose children have been hurt by coaches and team leaders through bullying, personal favoritism, and other injustices that can happen through sports. If Christian parents get involved, acting as the light and salt in school sports, their children will experience a much healthier and more rewarding experience, with less of the trauma that comes from a prideful, unjust spirit.

Here are some other ways a parent or guardian can get involved in their children's schools:

- Chaperon field trips or dances. If your child thinks it's just too embarrassing to have you on the dance floor, sell soft drinks down the hall from the dance.
- Serve on the school committees or advisory councils as a parent representative.
- Help on projects, such as editing the school newsletter.
- Help in your child's class, in the school library, in the cafeteria, or in the school office.
- Make food for a school event.
- Tutor students in areas such as reading, math, English, Spanish, computer skills, or other subjects.
- Work in a parent resource center or help start one. In these school centers, parents may gather informally, borrow materials on parenting and children's schoolwork, and get information about community service.[62]

The public-school environment is a minefield of positive and negative impacts. Socially, children are placed in an environment that does not reflect adult life. Considering the fact that children spend the majority of their time in the hands of public educators who may or may not hold the same values as the parent, it is imperative that parents keep a keen eye on the daily activities that go on in these institutions.

# 23

# <u>School Board</u>

FOR YEARS, MOTHERS TOOK FOR GRANTED that they could trust school officials, teachers, and school nurses. The last person a mother thought could be a threat to her children was a government official.

However, the political landscape has changed so radically in the last few years—changed for the worst—that it has provoked the Mama bears to the point that school officials, doctors, and government officials will soon be running, and possibly begging, for their professional lives.

Nothing can ever come between a mother and her children unless the spirit of the age deceives the mother and she surrenders her children out of ignorance. But with Mama grizzly bears—warrior women of God—that's not happening. If any of the above tries to come after their children, expect confrontation at every level.

Indeed, the conflicts have begun. The political left should have stayed away, kept their distance, remained in their corner, and respected their boundaries. Instead, they entered the familial caves uninvited and poked, prodded, and disturbed the natural order of family life. Big mistake!

The left has aroused the wrath of the Mama bears with Critical Race Theory (CRT) and sexual education that promotes sexual activities hidden from parental awareness and authority. Their goal is to dismantle the nuclear family.

As of this writing, in my state: Washington State, Governor Inslee approved legislation mandating critical race theory training for all public-school teachers. He also signed the most aggressive, perverted sex education bill in the nation.

The fight is on.

Across the nation, mothers are rising up against the brainwashing of their children. They are pushing back against the darkness. They are gathering together as a mighty force and with a strong, unified voice. They are forming alliances and showing up for their children and others in their communities. Mama bears are present at school board meetings and are jumping in for seats at the table of school boards. They are gathering on social media, sending emails, and making appearances at civil activities.

In a Federalist article, Carrie Benton writes:

> One Virginia mother, a Chinese immigrant, likened critical race theory to the abuses inflicted on the Chinese population during the Cultural Revolution and insisted it should have no place in our schools.

> A black mother, also from Virginia, called for the ban of critical race theory, which she slammed as an abusive tactic designed to divide and oppress. One Arizona mother had to point out the bleeding obvious that we should be teaching children about seeing and valuing humanity, not colors.

> A Colorado mother accused the Douglas County School District board of marginalizing parents and pushing equity and collectivism over equality of opportunity. She reminded them that their real job was not to engage in social engineering but to address the county's dismal proficiency in areas like reading and math. In a jaw-dropping ten-minute throw down, New York mother Tatiana Ibrahim blasted her school district for demoralizing children, teaching them communist values, undermining her family's religious beliefs, and encouraging hatred of and violence towards police officers. Ibrahim promised to become the school board's worst nightmare. [63]

According to America First Legal:

Local school boards make important decisions concerning curriculum, staffing, and budgeting for the nation's public schools. Depending on state laws, school boards have a direct influence on the quality of education students receive.

The Supreme Court has stated several times parents have the authority and responsibility over their children's education. And yet schools continue to ignore parents' rights. The administrators and teachers often treat parents with contempt and disdain simply for asking what their children are learning and what values schools promote.

Want to join the fight? Here is a powerful toolkit providing parents with the foundation for their legal rights in the school system:

## THE PROTECTION OF PUPIL RIGHTS AMENDMENT: A TOOLKIT FOR PARENTS

The Protection of Pupil Rights Amendment, 20 U.S.C. § 1232h, is one important—but until now little-used—tool for holding administrators and teachers accountable. First passed in 1974 and then expanded several times (most recently in 2002), the PPRA provides parents legal rights to review curriculum and, in some circumstances, to opt out of certain activities at any school that receives federal funding.

Some states have laws that empower parents directly to find out what local public teachers and administrators are doing. But it is essential to recognize that federal law allows parents to review curriculum and prevents schools from asking highly personal questions about students' sex lives, drug usage, and things of that nature without parental consent. Parents must be vigilant and willing to fight for their children; the PPRA should be a valuable tool.

** This is for your general informational purposes only. It is not legal advice and does not create an attorney-client relationship between you and A.F.L. **[64]

## WHAT DOES THE PPRA COVER?

The PPRA gives parents the right to review the curriculum used to teach their child at school. It also provides an even more extensive set of rights to inspect and opt out of specific surveys and studies that probe into the children's lives and attitudes.

### Curriculum

Parents have the right to inspect "any instructional material" used as part of the education curriculum for the student. The parent who wants to exercise this right must request the material; the school does not have to provide access to the material without being asked first. Parents should demand schools disclose teacher training materials designed to affect or direct student instruction as "instructional material."

### Surveys

Without parental consent, schools cannot require a student to answer questions about:

- Political beliefs or affiliations
- Mental problems or challenges
- Sexual behavior or attitudes
- Illegal, antisocial, self-incriminating, or demeaning behavior
- Critical appraisals of people with close family relationships
- Relationships with lawyers, physicians, and ministers
- Religious beliefs or practices
- Income level (unless it's asked simply regarding eligibility to participate in a program)

If the school wants to distribute or administer a survey created by an outside entity (not the school), the parent has the right to review the survey first, along with any supplemental material (including teacher's manuals) that comes with the survey. Again, the parent must request this; the school does not have to provide copies without being asked first. Critically, this applies to all gender and race-related materials.

Certain school districts have retained survey and data mining companies. These companies sell race-focused student and teacher surveys, data management tools, and training on systemic racism and oppression, white supremacy, implicit bias, gender issues, and intersectionality, often under the rubric of "Social-Emotional Learning." If parents are engaged and object, then this sort of material should not be forced on children. But if parents are disengaged and silent, the PPRA and other laws are ineffective.

### Personal information to be sold

Parents must be notified and given a chance to opt their child out any time the school is going to collect personal identifying information from their child when that information would then be sold. This includes the child's and the parents' names, home address, phone numbers, and Social Security numbers, as well as any other identifying information that could be connected to the student. (There is an exception if this is for the development of educational products for students or schools.) It is not clear whether racial and gender data mining that occurs under the "Social-Emotional Learning" rubric is subject to the PPRA's privacy provisions, but it is an issue parents should raise and explore.

### Physical examinations

Parents must be notified and given a chance to opt their child out of any invasive physical examinations that are not emergencies. The law considers an examination "invasive" if it involves exposure of private body parts or any insertion of an instrument into the body (other than hearing, vision, or scoliosis screening).

## WHO IS COVERED?

### Schools

The statute applies to any school that receives federal funding. Public schools receive federal funds in the form of various grants and program funds. Some private schools also receive federal funds if they participate in federal programs.

### Parents and Children

The statute provides rights to the parents so long as the child is under the age of 18. After the child turns 18, the rights of parents under the statute transfer to the now-adult student.

## WHAT DOES THE SCHOOL HAVE TO DO?

The school must provide the parents with a notification when it wants to ask students about any of the matters listed in the law—surveys about sensitive personal matters and personally-identifying information that would be sold. It should ask the parents for written consent for their child to participate in any study that the school is requiring. If the parents do not consent, then the school, in theory, is prohibited from requiring the child to participate.

The school is also required to come up with a set of standard policies that it will follow to notify parents and obtain consent when needed. The school needs to provide notification to the parents at least once per year.

Often, the school will provide notice at the beginning of the year, in a perfunctory or highly technical way, to meet its legal obligations but without providing parents with real, actionable information. Again, parent vigilance and engagement are critical.

## WHAT CAN PARENTS DO UNDER THE PPRA?

Parents can request information directly from their school district with something as simple as a letter or an email that says:

Under the Protection of Pupil Rights Amendment, 20 U.S.C § 1232h, I request the following:

Immediate access to all curriculum material, including teacher training materials, used in [specify class].

Copies of all surveys and related documents given to my child during the past school year, and copies of the opt-out notifications you provided to parents asking for information concerning or related to—

- political affiliations or beliefs of the student or the student's parent;
- mental or psychological problems of the student or the student's family;
- sex behavior or attitudes;
- illegal, antisocial, self-incriminating, or demeaning behavior;
- critical appraisals of other individuals with whom respondents have close family relationships (this should include all material related to "white privilege" or "anti-racism");
- legally recognized privileged or analogous relationships, such as those of lawyers, physicians, and ministers;
- religious practices, affiliations, or beliefs of the student or student's parent; or
- income (other than that required by law to determine eligibility for participation in a program or for receiving financial assistance under such program).

If schools do not fulfill their obligations under the PPRA, parents can report violations to the U.S. Department of Education using the form provided at https://studentprivacy.ed.gov/file-a-complaint. Complaints must be made within 180 days of the date of the violation.

## WHAT CAN THE U.S. DEPARTMENT OF EDUCATION DO?

The U.S. Department of Education is charged with investigating and adjudicating violations upon learning of a violation. The Secretary of Education can terminate a school's federal funding if the school has violated the law and refuses to voluntarily comply.

## WHAT CAN YOU DO IF THE U.S. DEPARTMENT OF EDUCATION REFUSES OR FAILS TO ACT?

Parents have various potential options if the U.S. Department of Education refuses or fails to act. These include:

- Suing the Department of Education, the offending school district, and the individuals involved.
- Filing an administrative petition asking the Department of Education to stop funding the offending school district.
- Asking your congressman or senator to investigate.
- Asking your state representative and your state attorney general to investigate.
- Engaging in direct political action, e.g., petitions, school board protests, state or local curriculum and survey transparency laws, and electing new school board members who will follow the law.

**Consult an attorney to discuss what makes sense for you.**

https://aflegal.org/guides/

All parents should become the government's worse nightmare when the government infringes on parental rights. Parenting and guarding the hearts and minds of our children is not for the fainthearted. Your home and family unit are the refuge and strong tower for children. Not every parent needs to run for the school board, but every parent needs to safeguard the family.

# 24

# State and National Government

HERE IN THE UNITED STATES OF AMERICA, our government is operated by three branches—the judicial, the legislative, and the executive. These correspond to the offices we commonly know as the Supreme Court, the Congress, and the Presidency. These three branches were designed by our founding fathers to act as a balance for each other, ensuring that no single branch gained too much power. To the framers of the Constitution, the number three must have seemed right—fewer branches and power could be consolidated; more branches and power would be hopelessly fragmented.

The number three is significant in many ways, chief among them the fact that we serve a triune God composed of the Father, Son, and Holy Spirit. Here are some more remarkable three-facts:

- Our planet is in the third orbit from the sun.
- There is the law of the thirds in painting and photography.
- There are three primary colors.
- In theater, literature, and music, there are often three main parts.
- We see in three dimensions—length, width, and depth.
- There are three means of heat transfer: radiation, conduction, and convection.
- There are three classifications of rock: igneous, metamorphic (or pyroclastic), and sedimentary.
- The triple point of water is in three phases: solid, liquid and vapor.

- There are three laws of motion and three laws of thermodynamics.
- Time is past, present, and future.

But the most significant way the number three is shown is that Jesus Christ our Lord was crucified, buried, and rose from the grave on the third day.

Three is a powerful number that obviously came from the mind of God. Did our founding fathers think about its origin when they formed our government? Possibly. So, where did they get the idea of three branches of government?

Our constitution was written by men who followed the writings of Charles de Secondat, Baron de Montesquieu. James Madison relied heavily upon Montesquieu's theory of the separation of powers when drafting the Constitution. Montesquieu argued that the best way to secure liberty and prevent a government from becoming corrupted was to divide the powers of government. But where did Montesquieu receive this initial truth of three branches? he got his ideas from a more famous philosopher, Aristotle. In Book IV Chapter 13 of his Politics, it reads,

> Having thus gained an appropriate basis of discussion we will proceed to speak of the points which follow next in order. All constitutions have three elements, concerning which the good lawgiver has to regard what is expedient for each constitution. When they are well-ordered, the constitution is well-ordered, and as they differ from one another, constitutions differ. There is (1) one element which deliberates about public affairs; secondly (2) that concerned with the magistracies—the questions being, what they should be over what they should exercise authority, and what should be the mode of electing to them; and thirdly (3) that which has judicial power.[65]

190

So, following the trail, where did Aristotle receive his information? Whatever writings he was studying, there is no question that the three branches of government came directly from the heart and mind of God.

*For the LORD is our judge, the LORD is our lawgiver, the*
*LORD is our king; it is he who will save us.*

Isaiah 33:22

Amazing isn't it? There it is—the three branches of government.

*For to us a child is born, to us a son is given, and the*
*government will be on his shoulders. And he will be called*
*Wonderful Counselor, Mighty God, Everlasting Father,*
*Prince of Peace. Of the greatness of his government and*
*peace, there will be no end. He will reign on David's throne*
*and over his kingdom, establishing and upholding it with*
*justice and righteousness from that time on and forever.*

Isaiah 9:6-7

Are there three branches of government in heaven? Well, there is the Father, Son, and Holy Spirit. The United States government is not perfect, but it definitely follows the pattern from Scripture. So, in our present time, it's workable.

The United States consists of federal government and state government. Government leaders vote on everything that involves our daily life. They vote on taxes, healthcare, transportation, marriage, distribution of goods, education and so much more. On the state level, the legislature will have 4 to 5 thousand bills to consider in each session. The responsibility is enormous. These two lists show governmental offices that are given by the voting public through elections and the other offices are given by appointment.

**Executive Branch—Carries Out Laws**

- President
- Vice president
- Cabinet—nominated by the president and must be approved by the Senate with at least fifty-one votes.

### Legislative Branch—Makes Laws

Congress is divided into two houses, the Senate and the House of Representatives.

- Senate—one hundred elected senators total, two senators per state.
- House of Representatives—435 elected representatives total, representatives based on each state's population.

### Judicial Branch-Evaluates Laws

- Supreme Court—nine justices nominated by the president and approved by the Senate with at least fifty-one votes.
- Federal courts
- State governments have the same three branches of government:
- Executive branch—governor
- Legislative branch—the Senate and House of Representatives
- Judicial branch—supreme court, superior court, tax court

These offices carry significant political weight. If a person aspires to lead in these federal or state offices, he or she must start at the community level.

- Establish a position in the local community as a mayor or city council member.
- Be involved in local elections, volunteer with local campaigns, and stay current on all the political hot topics in your state.
- Show up for rallies and parades.
- Volunteer at voting booths.
- Get to know the leaders in the political party that hold the same views.
- Get party support, and make friends and allies before deciding on running for office.

In addition to these steps, consider becoming a precinct committee officer (PCO). A PCO helps win city and state elections in a variety of ways. The most important is educating the people in the local district. A PCO builds up the community, shares information, and supports campaigns. They are a vital link to the party they serve.

Education is an important qualification for these higher offices. Almost all congresspeople have a bachelor's degree and many have master's degrees and law degrees. College is not a prerequisite to obtaining political office, but in actuality, the more educated a person is, the better equipped that person will be to serve the people and defend themselves against critics. Online education has made it easier to attain degrees and move up the ranks to achieve political aspirations.

If the Christian community begins to take hold of the importance of these positions, Christian families can change a community, a city, a state, and our nation. How do we do this? By bringing the political fire to the family first. Engage your children to think about becoming a Supreme Court judge, a senator, or a state treasurer.

From an early age, young people should think about changing the world through government. Becoming an intern is a great first step and has the potential to open doors for future careers. There are thousands of internships in government that can be filled. Many powerful people in government today started out as interns. Interns help with administration, running errands, writing, making phone calls, etc. They also help with research on issues that are up for vote or things that are needed for congressional hearings.

**Early Education**

An appreciation for these things needs to be instilled at a very young age. This can be done through family field trips to the state capitol, the White House, and the other places that show the strength of the government. It can also be fun to watch national elections with your family. One of the sweetest memories I will always treasure is the night of the 2016 national election. It was about 3:00 p.m., and I was wanting to watch the election, but according to the media, the election was already over before it began. So, I thought maybe I would skip watching. Then I heard someone turning a key in my front door. My sons are grown and out of the house, but they still have keys. It was my son, Nathanael.

"Hey, what are you doing here?" I asked. "Aren't you watching the election?" he said.

"No, not yet," I said.

"Well, let's get it on," he said.

"OK, have you had dinner yet?" (Of course, the mom thing kicks in.)

"No. Whatcha got?"

"I can make tacos." (His favorite.)

"YEAH! Let's do it."

So, I began cooking, and he turned on the television.

"I'm texting Jordan to see if he wants to join us," he said about my oldest son.

"Go for it," I said.

"Hey, Jordan wants to know if the tacos are chicken or beef."

"Chicken," I said.

"Are you making rice?"

"Of course, I'm making rice!"

"He'll be right over."

Jordan arrived within the hour. In the next hour, Andrew, the youngest of the three, came over too. The four of us sat and watched the 2016 election unfold. Nathanael had the remote and kept changing the channels back and forth to watch the different pundits' opinions. Watching how a United States president becomes elected was one of the greatest shows on Earth. The cable news shows made it more suspenseful by not calling the states too soon for fear of making a mistake. We watched the electoral map change from state to state. The energy that was pulsating through me was also going through my sons. We were all on the edge of our seats. My house was filled with awe observing the process, and once again I was given the opportunity to lead my home by answering questions, making comments on their observations, and bonding with my children on an adult level. It was electrifying. Why? Because I have been talking to my children about politics since they were in grade school. The seeds were planted very early.

> *This is what the Kingdom of God is like. A man scatters seed on the ground. Night and day, whether he sleeps or gets up, the seed sprouts and grows, though he does not know how. All by itself the soil produces grain—first the stalk, then the head, then the full kernel in the head. As soon as the grain is ripe, he puts the sickle to it, because the harvest has come.*

Mark 4:27-28

Plant your seeds early to become a public official on the state and national levels. Prepare the ground not only for this generation but for the next one ahead. The Church will reap a harvest of governmental leaders the world has yet to see.

# 25

# International

ON MAY 7, 2017, EIGHTY-THREE GIRLS WERE KIDNAPPED from a school in Nigeria by a group of militants called Boko Haram. The name means "western education is forbidden," and they are at war with the West and Christianity. The new leader of this militant group has vowed to bomb churches and kill off Christians in Nigeria.

However, attacks on Christians are not limited to Nigeria. According to the ministry Open Doors, North Korea has been No. 1 on the World Watch List—as the most dangerous country in the world for Christians—for 17 consecutive years. An estimated 80,000-130,000 political prisoners are kept in North Korea's prison camps. Prisoners in the camps are often "tortured and killed on account of their religious affiliation, with officials instructed 'to wipe out the seed of [Christian] reactionaries,'" and "in one account, guards killed a prisoner's newborn baby by feeding it to guard dogs." Further, routine public executions are carried out in front of both children and adults. These displays of cruelty are designed to subdue the prison population.[66]

Colombia, South America, is severely affected by corruption, with the main agents of persecution being leaders of criminal groups such as drug cartels and dissident guerrilla groups. Indigenous leaders also persecute Christians under suspicion of trying to impose their worldview for territorial advantage. Violent Christian persecution is commonplace in this South American country, both at the hands of criminal and indigenous groups. Guerrilla groups force Christians to pay a "protection tax"—which amounts to insurance against assault or murder. They issue death threats to Christians involved in evangelism, fearing that believers will continue to stand in opposition to the reign of terror these groups use to maintain power.

The fact is, there are many Christians all over the world being persecuted for their faith. The Open Doors ministry helps the Christian community with information on ways to help our brothers and sisters in these nations. One way to help is by rising up in governmental positions. The more governmental authority, the stronger the voice. Becoming a diplomat on the governmental scene is a powerful way to combat the persecutions. The next generation of ambassadors will need a strong, passionate vision for the whole world. They will need to be disciplined from an early age and pointed in the right directions to attain these important roles. According to Diplomacy 101, a U.S. diplomat's mission is to carry out the foreign policy of the United States. This is done in various ways.

Here is a list of what they do.

Our diplomats support Americans living or traveling internationally for positive events (such as registering a birth of a child) and in times of stress (such as assisting a jailed American citizen or helping to evacuate Americans from danger.)

- They ensure a level playing field for American businesses overseas.
- They support joint counterterrorism cooperation and criminal investigations.
- They decide who has a legitimate reason to travel to the United States and issue visas accordingly.
- They work to ensure the safety and security of international flights to the United States.
- They fight pandemics and deliver humanitarian aid to those in need.
- They assist governments to respond better to their citizens' needs, making countries more stable and secure.
- They link emerging leaders in government and civil society to American counterparts to foster relationship-building and collaboration.

Ambassadors are the chief officers under the United States president at embassies. Under the ambassador, five types of foreign service officers work together as a team.

- Economic (or "econ") officers work with foreign governments to secure internet freedom, fund scientific advances, protect the environment, or negotiate new trade laws.
- Management officers are action-oriented "go-to" leaders responsible for all embassy, consulate, or diplomatic mission operations from real estate to people to budget.
- Political officers keep the ambassador up-to-date on political events and changes occurring in the country.
- Public diplomacy officers build mutual understanding and support for U.S. policies by reaching directly to the public in foreign countries working with traditional and social media; websites; educational, cultural, and sports programs; and all manner of people-to-people exchange.

Consular officers' primary job is assisting and protecting American citizens abroad. If you lose your passport, find yourself in trouble with the law, or want to get married to a foreigner overseas, you'll need the help of this officer. Consular officers also issue visas to non-U.S. citizens who wish to travel, work, study, or live in the United States.[67] There are positions in government that can be attained, but they take years of planning and work. These positions are called diplomats. A person does not become a diplomat immediately out of college.

John Christopher Stevens, the Benghazi ambassador who served Libya, served only three and a half months before he was killed by militants in 2012. Before attaining that post, Stevens had this experience:

- He earned a B.A. in history in 1982 at the University of California, Berkeley.
- From 1983 to 1985, he taught English as a Peace Corps volunteer in Morocco.

- He graduated with a J.D. from the University of California, Hastings College of the Law in 1989.
- He received an M.S. degree from the National War College in 2010.
- Stevens was an international trade lawyer based in Washington, D.C.
- He was admitted as an active member of the State Bar of California on January 26, 1990.
- He went on inactive status on August 1, 1991 and remained an inactive member for the remainder of his career.
- Stevens joined the United States Foreign Service in 1991. His early overseas assignments included these:
- Deputy principal officer and political section chief in Jerusalem
- Political officer in Damascus
- Consular/political officer in Cairo and consular/economic officer in Riyadh.

In Washington, Stevens served as these:

- Director of the Office of Multilateral Nuclear and Security Affairs
- Pearson Fellow with the Senate foreign relations committee and Senator Richard Luga
- Special assistant to the undersecretary for political affairs
- Iran desk officer and staff assistant in the Bureau of Near Eastern Affairs.
- He had served in Libya twice previously: as the deputy chief of mission (from 2007 to 2009) and as special representative to the National Transitional Council (from March 2011 to November 2011) during the Libyan revolution.
- He arrived in Tripoli in May 2012 as the U.S. ambassador to Libya.

Stevens spoke English, French, and some Arabic.[68]

The goal of a Christian is to be an ambassador for Jesus Christ.

*We are therefore Christ's ambassadors, as though God were
making his appeal through us.*

2 Corinthians 5:20

If more Christians prepared themselves to become political
diplomats and officers for their countries, then many glorious gates
would open to these nations. The authority that is vested in these posts
allows for the Christians in these positions to call upon the Lord for
salvation, protection, and for guidance and strategies all over the world
to root out the evil forces. As stated above, these officers are up-to-date
on all political events and changes that occur in the country they are
assigned. I, like millions of other Christians, do not know when the
Lord is returning the second time. It may be a while. Therefore,
Christians need to understand what it would take to train their children
and grandchildren to aspire to these political posts. Becoming an
ambassador or a diplomat is a long and arduous process. In addition,
these positions are usually political appointments. The people who
receive these appointments have been involved in political circles and
have family, friends, and associates to turn to, to receive these
positions. Christians need to grab hold of this vision as a way of
changing the world. An ambassador to any nation is a gate of authority
and could do much good for the kingdom, especially if that ambassador
has a prophetic/evangelistic mantel. We need to train and raise up the
next generation of international prophets.

Prepare early to become a world changer. Instill the desire in your
children and grandchildren to become involved in international affairs.
Visit a local diplomat, ask questions, and find out exactly what the
starting points would be to go from desire to the actual execution. The
church is still the answer to all the world's deepest problems.

# Volume III

# The Church in Recent History

# Introduction to Volume III

JESUS'S DEATH, BURIAL, AND RESURRECTION BROUGHT FORTH the new church with a new mission. That mission was given to us in Matthew.

> *Go therefore and make disciples of all nations, baptizing them in the name of the Father and of the Son and of the Holy Spirit, teaching to observe all that I have commanded you.*

Matthew 28:19-20 (NKJV)

Since that mandate, untold millions have obeyed the Lord and walked in relationship with him. Throughout history, God, through his Holy Spirit, has released gifts to his people. These gifts are with people from all walks of life. They come out from the world and into the Kingdom of God, forming his church as it says in Ephesians 4.

God uses people to change the world; he delivers nations through people. This is how the world is advancing in goodness. When evil arises, God is there to push it back and bring forth the light of change. In many instances, the changes in our world happened through Christians. Bold and brave Christians with faith in God have changed the course of history, time and time again.

A perfect example is human slavery through the centuries. God is eradicating slavery, first by delivering his people from the slavery of sin, and then by continuing that deliverance in nations. It's amazing to witness the hand of God stretching out to human beings to deliver them from evil and set them free from sin.

The stories you are about to read are true stories. The men and women in these stories are people of faith. Faith in God brought movements in the earth, and these movements changed governments, laws, and culture. For many, it required persevering faith and strength, but God graced them and sustained them. We see God on the move through every generation. It's exciting because we know his love, goodness, and mercy endure. Nothing will stop God's eternal plan for humankind.

Nothing.

# 26

# Separation of Church and State

IF YOU ARE A PERSON OF FAITH and a civics student, you have heard people tell you that you're not allowed to practice your faith in schools, city, state government, and the public square. Why? Because, they say, the Constitution mandates a separation of Church and State. The result of this understanding is that people of faith cannot make decisions or raise questions about laws, guidelines, or rules if they use the Bible or other religious documents to state their arguments. Likewise, religious study, the Bible, and prayer are prohibited in public schools. Many Christian monuments and symbols have been removed. In our country, the "Separation of Church and State" is ingrained in today's culture. Untold thousands believe this is in the Constitution, but it is nowhere to be found. It is a distortion of a quotation from a letter written by one of the founding fathers: Thomas Jefferson.

Let's take a trip back into the history of the "Separation of Church and State." It's important to understand that this separation issue didn't begin with Thomas Jefferson in the United States.

The separation of Church and State started with God himself. If you are privileged to own a Founders Bible, you would see on page 683 where David Barton writes:

> When God established civil government for his people Israel, he placed Moses over the civil affairs and Aaron over the spiritual ones-the nation was one, but the jurisdictions were two, with separate leaders over each. The account of King Uzziah of Judah in 2 Chronicles 26 provides a lucid

illustration of how God insisted that the two jurisdictions be kept separate. Uzziah's reign lasted fifty-two years. Prosperity and stability characterized his civil rulership; his agricultural and animal husbandry programs were legendary; his national defense program was unrivaled.... His fame spread across the civilized world; his personal piety toward God was also well known, and he openly and boldly honored God throughout his kingdom. According to the Scriptures, all of this was highly commendable, but then a dramatic change occurred. The turning point is recorded in verse 16, with the revealing statement that Uzziah "entered the temple of the Lord to burn incense on the altar of incense." As a civil ruler over the kingdom, he decided that he would also take unto himself the function of a priest by burning incense on the altar; but that duty had been strictly reserved by God for his priests. Uzziah, by trying to perform the responsibilities of both Church and State and become the head in each, had thus crossed a line drawn by God Himself. Understanding this violation, the priests courageously and forcefully withstood him (v.18), but Uzziah refused to listen and became enraged at them. He seized their sacred utensils and prepared to make use of them when God weighed in: he instantly struck Uzziah with leprosy, who fled the temple in horror and humiliation. Significantly, it had been acceptable for Uzziah to honor God in his kingdom, and it had been acceptable for Uzziah to enter the temple to worship God. But when Uzziah attempted to violate the jurisdictional separation between State and Church-when he sought to be in charge of both the civil and religious arenas at the same time-God provided a dramatic precedent as a message of warning to all future generations.[69]

God Himself separated the Civil from the Priesthood, and the separation of Church and State is from the heart of God. Civil servants and civil authority have an anointing and calling from God, as well as

Church servants and leaders, and both are ordained and created by the Lord's wisdom and power.

As time passed, national leaders lusted for power and control and began to mingle the two. This mingling brought a dilution of spiritual power and holiness in the Church. One of the most blatant examples was King Henry VIII when he separated from the Catholic Church because the pope would not grant him a divorce so that he could remarry. Instead of honoring the church rules of his time, he started his Church called the Anglican Church. This new Church was a combination of State and Church, and Henry gave himself a divorce under this new spiritual jurisdiction.

His daughter Elizabeth followed her father's governmental ways and became the head of the State and the Church, but she was more lenient toward the Protestant movement than her father at the beginning of her reign. The State was entirely in charge of the Church. This Church was called the Church of England. According to David Barton:

> "The Church existed by permission of the civil government. If you lived or were born within a certain radius of a Church of England, you were automatically a member from birth to death and billed or tithed accordingly. The Church of England was the only Church supported by taxpayers. The government controlled the Church, and the Church controlled the people."

Amid this controlled religious state, a movement of true believers was rising. With access to the Bible, these believers realized God established the Church and made a covenant with the members of his body. They discovered the state church's corruption and knew it needed reform. True believers became part of a movement called the Reformation. From this movement came the Puritan movement, which spawned another group called the Separatists. The Separatists believed in the separation of the Church from the State. Again, the separation came from the Lord's people, not the State. A prominent Revered named John Greenwood led a church of many of the Pilgrims. Greenwood argued that there could be but one head to the Church and that its head was not the queen but Christ. He was executed for his stand. Laws were passed after this incident punishing those who called for separation.

Many left England for religious freedom. Once they arrived on American soil, they purposed in their hearts that the civil government would never rule in the life of the Church again. The pilgrims even started their own civil code of conduct called the Mayflower Compact. Through the years, different churches and religions emerged throughout the colonies. The common thread with them was that the government would never have the power to rule in their churches or their forms of worship.

When the Constitution of the United States was written, the first amendment began with these words:

> "Congress shall make no law respecting an establishment of religion or prohibiting the free exercise thereof."

This amendment was designed to prohibit the State from interfering with or suppressing the religious expression of citizens in private or public. Thomas Jefferson understood this and agreed. He received a letter from the Danbury Baptist Association with concerns about the government trying to regulate them. Jefferson reassured the Baptist Association with these words.

> That religion is a matter which lies solely between man and his God; that he owes account to none other for his faith or his worship; that the legislative powers reach actions only and not government opinions, I contemplate with sovereign reverence that act of the whole American people which declared that their legislature should "make no law respecting an establishment of religion or prohibiting the free exercise thereof" [the First Amendment], thus building a wall of separation between Church and State. [70]

The above paragraph was a response to a letter from Jefferson confirming that there is a wall and that wall protects the Church. That wall keeps the government out of the Church, not the Church out of the government.

# 27

# William Wilberforce

WILLIAM WILBERFORCE WAS CALLED AND APPOINTED BY GOD to abolish slavery. Through his aunt and uncle, he converted to Christianity and was brought under the influence of great Christian men like George Whitefield and John Newton. John Newton was involved in the slave trade, and after his conversion, he wrote the hymn *Amazing Grace.* The abolitionists of his day were passionate. They held the fire of freedom in their hearts, but William Wilberforce knew he was appointed to end slavery. So he began that process early in his life. He had a burning desire to see this task through before his complete conversion to Christ.

In his college years, he turned from his faith and went about living life on his own. Because he was born into wealth, he made friends easily and entertained them well. After college, he wasn't sure what to do in his life. His friend William Pitt was groomed from a young boy to enter Parliament. Both men became best friends. William Pitt encouraged Wilberforce to go into politics.

At last, William sensed a deep purpose for his life and entered the political arena. He was elected to Parliament in September 1780 at the age of 21. His friend William Pitt eventually became Britain's Prime Minister. Pitt and Wilberforce were inseparable and worked together on many issues in Parliament. Both men were passionate speakers.

Wilberforce participated in Parliament and became one of Parliament's leading debaters, although Christ Jesus was not yet at the forefront of his mind and heart. Then something happened. He went on a trip through Europe and invited Isaac Milner, an Anglican clergyman, to accompany him. Isaac was also a scientist and mathematician. Through his knowledge and intellect, Milner immersed William in the teachings of Jesus Christ and the Christian worldview. They studied the Greek New Testament and other Christian writings to the point that Wilberforce became convicted of his sin, and so he converted.

His conversion was so strong that he considered leaving Parliament because of the nature of politics. His desire leaned toward ministry, but his friend William Pitt persuaded him to stay in government. Pitt said, "Surely the principles as well as the practice of Christianity are simple, and lead not to meditation only but to action."

William began to work with a team to end the slave trade in England. Ending the slave trade would make it illegal to purchase kidnapped Africans and transport them around the world to plantations, where they were treated harshly and worked to death. William helped by giving the team access to shipping records kept in the government Customs House. The purpose of studying these records was to get accurate numbers of the enslaved people that died on ships during the "Middle Passage."

The "Middle Passage" was a voyage to the West Indies that took three to four weeks. Because the ships went right through the tropical belt, the heat in these ships was unbearable. A 100-150 tons vessel could carry 300-600 enslaved people. They placed the enslaved people so close together that they could barely move or breathe.

William Wilberforce began his cause to end slavery, but another cause close to his mind and heart was the cause to reform society. His conversion to Christianity opened his eyes, and he saw the need for moral living. At the same time, King George III also issued a proclamation that ended gambling on Sunday. He called for the prosecution of excessive drunkenness, violent outbursts, and other harmful behaviors. William encouraged morals and began societies of moral and good manners.

William introduced his first bill in 1789 to abolish the slave trade. He gave an impassioned speech and spoke for over three hours. He described the horrors of the Middle Passage, how over 400 people were fitted below deck on a ship, and the terrible conditions upon those trips. He ended his first speech to abolish the slave trade with these words.

> The nature and all the circumstances of this Trade are now laid open to us. We can no longer plead ignorance, we cannot evade it, it is now an object placed before us, we cannot pass it. We may spurn it, we may kick it out of our way, but we cannot turn aside so as to avoid seeing it. For it is brought now so directly before our eyes that this House must decide, and must justify to all the world, and to their own conscience, the rectitude's of their grounds and of the principles of their decision.... Let not Parliament be the only body that is insensible to national justice.[71]

The bill failed. Then, in 1791, his motion to abolish the slave trade lost 163-88. In 1793, he proposed a bill in the House of Commons advocating gradual abolition. It too failed by eight votes and most members didn't show up for the vote. After that, he brought forward a bill prohibiting British ships from carrying slaves to foreign territories. It lost by two votes and again with many members not in attendance.

Wilberforce reintroduced the Abolition Bill almost every year in the 1790s. Every year it failed. And yet, he continued to persevere.

A person must believe in their purpose to persevere through so many failures. Fighting the good fight and standing for what you believe, against monumental odds, causes the changes to happen. It was time to end slavery, and there was grace on Wilberforce to do it. The grace was not only on Wilberforce but on thousands around the world to break the chains of slavery.

Some would argue that slavery was all through the Bible and perfectly acceptable, but in the Christian's heart and mind, and according to conscience, the will of God was against kidnapping human beings and enslaving them. God came forth through Wilberforce to change the world.

Each generation has a mandate from God. Failure is not an excuse to stand down but a requirement to keep standing according to scripture. And while we stand, God sends strength and encouragement in and through the battle.

In 1791, John Wesley, the fiery preacher and founder of the Methodist Movement, wrote William a letter.

> I see not how you can go through your glorious enterprise in opposing that execrable villainy, which is the scandal of religion, of England, and of human nature. Unless God has raised you up for this very thing, you will be worn out by the opposition of men and devils. But if God be for you, who can be against you? Are all of them stronger than God? Oh be not weary in well doing! Go on, in the name of God and in the power of his might, till even American slavery (the vilest that ever saw the sun) shall vanish away from it. Reading this morning a tract [written] by a poor African, I was particularly struck by that circumstance that a man who has a black skin, being wronged or outraged by a white man, can have no redress: it being a "law" in our colonies that the oath of black against a white goes for nothing. What villainy is this? That he who has guided you from youth up may continue to strengthen you in this and all things, is the prayer of, dear sir,
>
> Your affectionate servant,
>
> John Wesley.[72]

This was the last letter John Wesley ever penned.

William knew that ending the slave trade would only come about through the power of God. The British Empire was one of the largest empires that extended worldwide. It went from England to Canada, through the United States, into the Orient, then down into the South Seas, South American, Central America, and throughout Africa. Millions of enslaved people were held throughout the empire, and in most businesses and enterprises, slavery had its tentacles.

Wilberforce had the faith and tenacity to end it, but it would take all of his life to do it. It took over two decades to end the slave trade in England. During that time of presenting bills to end the slave trade year after year, William worked on his other passions for Christ. Because of his vast wealth inherited from his father and uncle, he could work and give himself to many volunteer societies, church work, and philanthropic efforts. Wilberforce said, "God has set before me two great objects, the suppression of the slave trade and the reformation of manners." His ambition was to "Make Goodness Fashionable."

According to Richard Gathro:

> One historian has calculated that Wilberforce was a member of the committee of some sixty-nine voluntary societies. In addition to his abolition work, he was consistently involved in church work that included the Church Missionary Society and the sending of missionaries to India and Africa, the British and Foreign Bible Society, the Proclamation Society Against Vice and Immorality, the School Society, the Sunday School Society, the Society for Bettering the Condition of the Poor, the Vice Society and others. His public philanthropic efforts were many, including relieving the suffering of the manufacturing poor, and French refugees and foreigners in distress. History records Wilberforce as having made major financial contributions to at least seventy such societies, and as being active in numerous reform movements which included reform in hospital care, fever institutions, asylums, infirmaries, refugees and penitentiaries. He supported religious publications and education, especially the schools of Hannah More, a close friend and leading reformer of British education.

Wilberforce didn't set out on any of these projects alone. According to Gathro:

Wilberforce and his closest friend, Henry Thornton, called together a group of Christians with the desire to apply their faith in Jesus Christ to personal, social, political, national, and international matters.

The group was called the Clapham sect. The group did not claim to be theologians, yet they regarded prayer and Bible study as serious matters. The Clapham group believed they were representatives of God's kingdom on earth and the faithful stewards of all God had given them. Together, this Clapham fellowship sought to make the British Empire an instrument of social and moral welfare for all people. Throughout their time together, they remained remarkably committed to these goals.

Perhaps this circle of friends can best be remembered by these characteristics:

- They shared a common commitment to Jesus Christ and a clear sense of calling.

- They were committed to lifelong friendship and mutual submission was the norm.

- Their advocacy was marked by careful research, planning and strategy.

- They worshiped both privately and publicly, gathering twice weekly at the Clapham Church.

- Their friendships were inclusive and focused on the essentials. For example, Wilberforce was a Wesleyan and his closest friend, Henry Thornton, was a Calvinist.

- They made family life a clear priority and delighted in each other's marriages and children.

- They kept the "long view" on completing projects. Abolition of the slave trade took 20 years!

- They made no dichotomy between evangelism and social action. Their magazine, The Christian Observer, exemplifies this.

- Their faith was integral to all of life...family, career, friendship and more. It was a faith that the younger generation calls, "24/7." They talked together of a faith that impacted every part of their lives. There were no "compartments."

- They enabled one another vs. trying to "have it all."[73]

- They recognized each other's passions and supported one another in addressing them.

Finally, in 1807, the bill for the Abolition of the Slave Trade went into the House again with a passionate speech. This time, abolitionists introduced the bill to the House of Lords first instead of the House of Commons. The bill passed the House of Lords by a vote of 100 for and 36 against. When the bill went to the House of Commons, several MPs gave speeches and mentioned Wilberforce's name. They gave him a standing ovation. William wept in his hands and cried out to God in thankfulness. The House of Commons passed the bill 283 to 16. It finally happened. The slave trade was banished from the British Empire.

Ending the slave trade, however, was different than abolishing slavery from the entire British empire. The law stopped the slave trade with England, but slavery was still legal. Banning the slave trade meant British ships could no longer go to Africa and take human beings on slave ships, but the English colonies still enslaved people. Wilberforce was not content to just ending British slave ships but putting an end to slavery entirely. He never gave up on that dream and continued to work and contribute to ending slavery and several other noble causes. It would take another twenty-six years to end slavery in the British Empire. During those twenty-six years, a new generation of abolitionists rose up to fight the good fight. In 1833, a retired Wilberforce gave one last speech in Parliament to put slavery to an end. On July 26th, 1833 slavery ended in Britain. William Wilberforce fulfilled his dream. He died three days later.

# 28

# Harriet Beecher Stowe

"God wrote Uncle Tom's Cabin," Harriet told a friend. "I only put down what I saw [...] It all came before me in visions, one after another, and I put them down in words."

By the eve of the war, as one Southerner of the day noted, the novel:

"...had given birth to a horror against slavery in the Northern mind which all the politicians could never have created." And it "did more than all else to array the North and South in compact masses against each other."[74]

It is reported that upon being introduced to Harriet Beecher Stowe in 1862, Abraham Lincoln fondly commented she was "the little woman who wrote the book that started this great war."

Most notably, the popular Southern author, Thomas Dixon, attended an Uncle Tom play in 1901 and was so infuriated by what he regarded as its endorsement of black power that he wrote bitterly of Stowe:

A little Yankee woman wrote a book. The single act of that woman's will caused the war, killed a million men, desolated and ruined the South, and changed the history of the world.[75]

Harriet was born and raised in a minister's home. Her father and brothers were ministers, and Harriet was a strong Christian who underwent several transformations in her faith. She brought her faith and religion into almost everything she wrote. These stories affected the hearts and minds of her readers. The emotions of fear, anger, love, and hate came through her writings, connecting the emotional being with the Christian soul and spirit. Her writings convicted the conscience through simple everyday stories. Even when writing to friends, her faith came out strong. She was quoted as saying, "Indeed, I can barely keep my letters from turning into sermons." Her writing contained realism with inspirational messages.

She lived in the North and among strong, faithful Christian abolitionists. Abolitionists wrote speeches and sermons and debated incessantly on the evils of slavery. Harriet agreed with all of the views. But when her son Charley died, the pain she endured was compared in her heart to the pain of separation that slave mothers endured when their children were sold off. This tragic incident in her life, along with the Fugitive Slave Law, caused her to cry out as a parent. Slavery in the South was horrific for the family. Many southern owners cared little about selling precious mothers' children to other owners. These sales meant that the mother would never see her children again. It was wicked and cruel.

According to David S. Reynolds, in *Mightier Than The Sword*:

> Stowe decided that the institution of slavery could be gotten rid of only if the nation faced up to its sins. Politics had failed to wipe out slavery, and so had speeches, sermons, and all other forms of persuasion. Even fiction had failed when it took an openly subversive stance, as in the case of Hildreth's Archy Moore. What was needed was a novel that appealed to what a great leader calls 'the better angels of our nature.' *Uncle Tom's Cabin* gave America iconic angels in the form of a white girl and an enslaved black who died for the redemption of others. It unsparingly exposed the toil that slavery took upon blacks and whites, who were bonded by a common humanity. It put aside reformist wrangles, political squabbles, and sectional tensions… Written in protest against a nefarious law, *Uncle Tom's Cabin* accomplished what Lincoln said was more important than making statures: it molded public opinion. And it did so with a vigor unmatched by any other American novel.[76]

The nefarious law that Stowe wrote against was called the Fugitive Slave Law. The Fugitive Slave Law of 1850 did several things. Fugitives no longer had access to a trial by jury in state and local courts when their slave owners caught them. It required northerners to participate in the pursuit and apprehension of suspected runaways. It also added that anyone convicted of helping a runaway slave with food or shelter was subject to six months imprisonment and a $1000 fine. The law expanded federal powers by empowering federal commissioners and using federal marshals.

Then in March of 1857, the Dred Scott decision came down from the Supreme Court. The court decided that a slave could never sue for his freedom, and no black person, free or enslaved, could become a citizen, In addition, they also decided that Congress could not prohibit slavery in any territory. New laws were written up every week concerning slavery. In April of 1857, Sam Green, a conductor of the Underground Railroad, was tried and convicted of possessing a copy of *Uncle Tom's Cabin*. He received a ten-year sentence, and after serving five years, he was pardoned by the Governor of Maryland, Augustus Bradford, in 1862.

Harriet's book was considered literature that defied the Constitution. Well...she and other abolitionists believed in a higher law—God's law of justice and morality. Her brother, Charles, wrote a sermon called, "The Duty of Disobedience to Wicked Laws." After reading the novel, people in the North felt empowered to obey their conscience and break the Fugitive Slave Law. Harriet's book showed the depth of how far people would go to protect slaves and help them regardless of what slavery laws existed. The novel fostered and escalated breaking the law while appealing to the higher law of mercy and justice. Stowe's novel showed compassionate northerners working to free slaves and displayed the operations of the merciless slave trade in the South.

According to Stowe:

> The cruelty of proslavery laws that make possible the sale of enslaved men and women as chattel, trading negros from Africa, dear reader, is horrid, but trading them in Kentucky- that's quite another thing."

According to Reynolds:

> A historian of the domestic slave trade estimates that between 1790 and 1860 approximately one million African-Americans were transported from the Upper South to the Deep South, about two-thirds of them as a result of sale. Many were sold repeatedly. Tom's being sold three times, was by no means beyond probably.[77]

Stowe and other abolitionists held firm that slavery was an evil institution that needed evisceration. She stood firm with her convictions and worked tirelessly with other abolitionists to defend her views and novel. She sent copies of her novel to many politicians and spoke antislavery messages wherever the doors opened up for her. During that time, women were not at the forefront of politics, but that didn't stop Stowe. According to Reynolds,

> In 1854, the Tribune published her *Appeal to the Women of the Free States of America on the Present Crisis in Our Country*, exhorting women to pray, petition, and arrange events to stop a bill that she said would lead to the nationalization of slavery. Her bold statements didn't sit well with pro-slavery politicians. As one of Stowe's contemporaries wrote, "Uncle Tom's Cabin penetrated the walls of Congress and made the politicians tremble. It startled statesmen who scented danger near."[78]

The novel penetrated the walls of government and infused itself with culture, art, and everyday life. It became a phenomenon. The theatrical play based on the book launched thousands into the performing arts, including black performers and singers. To this day, it is the longest-running play in American history. Uncle Tom was in everything: games, products, paintings, dishware, cross-stitch, toys, and figurines. Uncle Tom was everywhere.

Uncle Tom was one of the most beloved novels and also one of the most hated. Southerners despised Stowe, and up to the 20th-century, authors and film makers were still combating Stowe's novel. The novel, *Gone with the Wind*, and the movie, *Birth of a Nation*, were created in part to sway public opinion against what the South perceived as propaganda and gross exaggerations of how the South treated slaves. The *Birth of a Nation* was based on novels written by Thomas Dixon. Three novels in the Klan trilogy—*The Leopard's Spots*, *The Clansman*, and *The Traitor*, used Stowe's characters and reversed them. The books praised the KKK and made the black man the aggressor and abuser. These books and movies swayed millions of people to sympathize with the South.

The book brought to the surface the deep hatred and bitterness of racism. And to this day, Uncle Tom is still in the mouths of our nation. Now, the term Uncle Tom today means something derogatory. It's simply amazing what God did through the heart of one of his followers. God did indeed write that novel through Stowe. Through one of his many faithful vessels, he crushed the most vile practice in United States history.

# 29

# Harriet Tubman and the Underground Railroad

AT FIVE YEARS OLD, HARRIET TUBMAN (a slave) was hired by another family to work indoors. She was asked to spin flax on a wheel. With no knowledge or training on the wheel, the little girl could barely hold on to the tight thread that ripped through her little hands. Being a slave during these pre-Civil War days brought pain, torture, punishment, and hunger. Many enslaved black people were treated worse than animals. Little Harriet was whipped simply because she didn't know or understand what she was asked to do. She was taken from that house and placed with another cruel, wicked family that whipped her mercilessly for not knowing how to beat the dirt out of a rug. Yet God had mercy on this little girl. She was eventually taken out of the second home and brought to work in the fields. The work was hard, but she could work without being watched over every hour.

While working in the field, she overheard friends and other field workers discussing freedom and a special train on the Underground Railroad. She was young and thought the railroad carried an actual train to freedom. In time, she would learn what the Underground Railroad was and what it did.

According to the National Geographic Society:

> During the era of slavery, the Underground Railroad was a network of routes, places, and people that helped enslaved people in the American South escape to the North. The name "Underground Railroad" was used metaphorically, not literally. It was not an actual railroad, but it served the same

purpose—transporting people long distances. It did not run underground but through homes, barns, churches, and businesses. The people who worked for the Underground Railroad had a passion for justice and a drive to end the practice of slavery—a drive so strong that they risked their lives and jeopardized their freedom to help enslaved people escape from bondage and keep them safe along the route. According to some estimates, between 1810 and 1850, the Underground Railroad helped to guide one hundred thousand enslaved people to freedom. As the network grew, the railroad metaphor stuck. "Conductors" guided runaway enslaved people from place to place along the routes. The places that sheltered the runaways were referred to as "stations," and the people who hid the enslaved people were called "station masters." The fugitives traveling along the routes were called "passengers," and those who had arrived at the safe houses were called "cargo.[79]

Harriet and many other slaves dreamed of their freedom and prayed every day that they could escape to the North. A good friend of Harriet's, Jim, told Harriet in secret that he was planning to escape. Jim eventually took off, and an overseer caught sight of Jim running. Harriet was so worried about Jim that she began running after him. All three ended up running into a store. The overseer ordered Harriet to help him tie up Jim, but Harriet refused. She even stood in the way while Jim ran out of the store. The man became so angry, he picked up a two-pound weight and threw it at Jim. I stead of hitting Jim, however, the iron weight hit Harriet, breaking her skull. She was bedridden for months. She suffered from severe headaches and blackouts for the rest of her life.

Harriet was exposed to Christianity at a very young age. According to Katherine Clifford Larson:

The role that evangelical Protestantism played in the lives of nineteenth-century slaves, particularly those in the region where Harriet lived in her formative years, is crucial to understanding the elements of Tubman's spiritual strength and endurance. Religion was a major support system within the African American community, for both the free and the enslaved...

When Harriet went into her blackouts, she had visions and visitations from God. She believed the sleeping spells were a portal from God. She would wake up from these spells with visions that prophesied the future. God began to personally speak and direct her life.

Sarah Bradford wrote of Harriet, "I hardly know how to approach the subject of the spiritual experiences my sable heroine. They seem to enter into the realm of the supernatural...Had I not... seen such remarkable instances of what seemed to be her direct intercourse with heaven, I should not dare risk my character for veracity by making these things public in this manner."[80]

While working in the field, Harriet talked, prayed, and dreamed about her freedom. She would look up to the stars and ask God to lead her out of the wicked chains of darkness. Through faith, she decided to escape. Her first departure took her through two states that encompassed 120 miles. She traveled at night with the guidance of the night star and received directions from those on her side. God led her through the night in dreams and visions and warned her of what people and places to avoid. The Holy Spirit led her through every step and kept her from the slave catchers and their hound dogs.

Harriet made it safely to Pennsylvania. She was free at last. Her heart burst with joy and sorrow. Joy because she made it to freedom. Her dream had finally become a reality. But sorrow because all the people she loved were enslaved. She was alone in her freedom. She decided to return to the South, save her family and friends, and bring them to freedom. Within eighteen months of her escape, Harriet recused six people from slavery: her niece, two children, her brother, and two other young men.

Returning to the South to deliver her family was hazardous due to the Fugitive Slave Law. The law made it more difficult for runaway slaves to retreat into the northern states. Slave owners now had the federal government's full support, and they hired ruthless bounty hunters to capture their runaways. Harriet's courage and faith, however, didn't let the new law stop her from returning to the South to deliver more people. After successfully saving some of her family, her faith and confidence grew. She became a conductor on the Underground Railroad. She evolved into a leader and soldier in the fight against slavery and was no longer a slave, but a warrior, a hero.

Her skills as a conductor eventually brought all of her family to freedom, including her aging parents. For almost a decade, she avoided capture and returned as often as resources would allow. She became a public speaker against slavery and was named "Moses" by her people. She trained and helped new conductors and showed them the exact routes and places to stop along the way. Her public speaking kept her audience spellbound with her stories and helped finance a farm with a house, barn, and other buildings. She walked with the Lord so closely that he showed her the United States would go to war. Many of her abolitionist friends scoffed at the thought that war could come and bring an end slavery but Harriet was adamant that war would surely come…and it did.

As a leader in the anti-slavery movement, Harriet's leadership brought her into relationships with the leading abolitionists of her day. She became acquainted with people such as:

- William Lloyd Garrison (outspoken abolitionist, journalist, suffragist, and social reformer)
- Frederick Douglass (National leader in the abolitionist movement, social reformer, orator, writer, and statesman)

- Sojourner Truth (Abolitionist, evangelist, and women's rights activist)
- William Still (Conductor on the Underground Railroad, abolitionist, businessman, writer, historian, and civil rights activist)
- Lucretia Mott (Abolitionist, pacifist, social reformer, and feminist activist who helped launch the women's rights movement)

This group formed a strong network of abolitionists who fought together and separately to end slavery.

Harriet's prophecy came to pass. In 1861 the Civil War began. Because of Harriet's successful record of leading slaves to freedom as a conductor, John Andrew, the governor of Massachusetts, asked her to be a spy for the Union Army. She arrived in Beaufort, South Carolina, in 1862. But instead of espionage work, Harriet was assigned to the Christian Commission, an operation established by the YMCA. The Christian Commission supplied and distributed food, clothing, blankets, books, and Bibles to the soldiers.

From that post, she was transferred to work with the sick and dying. She was assigned to a doctor named Henry K. Durant. Soldiers died both from combat wounds and diseased such as yellow fever and cholera. Because Harriet was raised on herbal remedies, she was a tremendous asset to the Union Army, and her medicines became known throughout the military camps. She also opened an "eating house" for the soldiers and workers. Harriet found the best prices for her baked goods and made pies and gingerbread. By day, she healed the sick; by night, she baked food to feed the hungry.

She gathered information from the soldiers and freedmen and found out where the Confederates were stationed and their next plan of action. She gave this information to the Union Army.

One of her most important missions involved cutting off supplies to Southern soldiers. She also rescued many slaves by ship. Her group decimated homes, barns, and storehouses serving the Confederate army, while saving almost 750 enslaved people. She continued for three years. After the war, Harriet continued to speak, advocating for civil rights, including the rights of women.

Frederick Douglass wrote of her:

> The difference between us is very marked. Most of what I have done and suffered in the service of our cause has been in public, and I have received much encouragement every step of the way. You, on the other hand, have labored in a private way. I have wrought in the day-you in the night. I have had the applause of the crowd and the satisfaction that comes with being approved by the multitude, while the most that you have done has been witnessed by a few trembling, scarred, and foot-sore bondmen and women whom you have led out of the house of bondage, and whose heartfelt "God bless you" has been your only reward. The midnight sky and the silent stars have been the witnesses of your devotion to freedom and your heroism. Excepting John Brown-of sacred memory-I know of no one who has willingly encountered more perils and hardships to serve our enslaved people than you have.

# 30

# Frederick Douglass

Before his childhood ended, Fredrick had decided that God was not responsible for his enslavement. It was his first momentous theological conviction, and perhaps the most important one of his life.[81]

FREDRICK DOUGLASS WAS BORN INTO SLAVERY on the Eastern shore in Talbot County. In his first seven years, he was raised by his grandmother. As a young boy, he was loved and nurtured. But his first devastation came when he was stripped from the arms of a loving family and taken to serve in a master's house.

Throughout his life, Douglass deployed many religious arguments against slavery. But the one that moved him most deeply was the cruel fact that slavery disregarded "all just ideas of the sacredness of the family, as an institution. He could only lament that his mother, like some many enslaved women, had many children, but no family."[82] According to Frederick, white masters did not regard the black mother and her love for children. She was looked upon as a breeder. The slave family was bought and sold many times over. Many children would be ripped from their mothers, never to be seen again.

Many white Southerners were church-going Methodists and even allowed the slaves to hear sermons on Sundays. Frederick observed that these masters and their wives attended church on Sunday, worshipping God and learning scripture about God's love, only to come back Monday through Saturday to beat, maim, and in many instances, rape their slaves. Frederick witnessed vicious beatings and murders—things that shocked him and caused him to wonder why some people are slaves and other people were masters. As he heard from the white master that God is love and he is good, Frederick began to question why God allowed some people to be slaves. How could a good, loving God allow such evil, barbaric acts?

Frederick asked these questions to other enslaved people. One of the answers he received was that it was God's design to make white people masters and black people slaves; that God knew what was best for everyone. This argument confused Frederick, and why wouldn't it?

The scripture taught that Christ Jesus came to give life, and life more abundantly, and that Satan comes to steal, kill and destroy. Frederick, who was not a learned man of scriptures at that time, cried out to God for understanding. The claim that a good God ordained certain people to slavery baffled Fredrick even more. The idea that God was responsible for slavery "pained me greatly," Douglass explained. He "wept over it long and often."[83]

Eventually, Fredrick crafted his own theodicy—his own justification of God's mysterious ways. Why were so many people trapped in bondage? It was not color, but crime—not God, but man— that afforded the true explanation of the existence of slavery. He blamed his enslavement not on an indifferent or malicious God but on human beings freely acting in greedy, oppressive, evil ways. Frederick reached this conclusion, in large part, by learning about slaves taken directly from Guinea, men and women, "stolen from Africa, forced from their homes, and compelled to serve as slaves." After hearing their stories, Douglass said, "the whole mystery was solved at once." God had not ordained these Africans to be slaves from birth. They were born free, and only later, due to the avarice of other men, were they enslaved.[84]

These conclusions could only come from God the Father. God revealed to Frederick his (God's) goodness and love. The Lord gave him discernment between good and evil, and in the years following, Frederick discerned the difference between God's love through the gospel and the demons' doctrines in churches. Knowing that it was not

God's will for him to be a slave caused him to cry out from his heart for his freedom.

Frederick learned to read, and the Bible became one of the books he read and cherished. He grew in his faith and knowledge and could see the utter hypocrisy of white Southerners' religion. On Sunday, they appeared pious and holy, and then they came home to sheer brutality with whippings, starvations, and cruelty that Frederick could not comprehend. Were their white masters truly Christians? How could they be when they showed no mercy to their slaves? They considered their slaves brute beasts, yet even the Heavenly Father wouldn't want animals to be treated with such cruelty. Time and time again, Frederick witnessed the opposite of what was preached on Sunday. Ministers preached against fornication and yet condoned the breeding of a woman slave with different men. Even the masters had sexual relations with their slave women, only to show up on Sunday with their Bible in one arm and their wives on the other.

Another grievous hypocrisy was that masters professed Christ as Lord and believed all men should be saved, but they disallowed slaves from reading the Bible. Those who could read were forbidden to go to God's word.

Douglass studied the Bible but also found a book called, *The Columbian Orator*. Through study, deep thought, and prayer, he realized that slavery was not God's will and that God didn't require him to submit to slavery in false humility and weakness. His faith grew, and there came a day when he believed that he would not be a slave forever. That faith grew into a reality, and through trials and tribulations, he became a free man.

Douglass and his wife began their free journey in New Bedford, Massachusetts. He wanted to connect to a Christian church and decided to find a Methodist church since Methodist believers gave him his foundation in faith. He first attended Elm Street Methodist Church. It was a white-led church. Yet Douglass was disappointed and disillusioned with how they separated the white believers from the black believers. They also ministered communion in a condescending form. After ministering communion to the white members, the leadership then allowed the black members to come forward. It was very telling to Douglass because he knew in his heart the Lord had no distinction of color when receiving communion. He saw the root of racism even in the church, and it grieved him.

Douglass eventually discovered the AME Zion Church of New Bedford and settled there as a member. He served as a sexton, steward, class leader, and clerk for the congregation. He started his public speaking at AME. He was blessed with strong oratory skills and learned how to express his beliefs in God and anti-slavery. Because Douglass believed that God did not establish slavery, his main message was aimed at destroying that belief system. He had no patience for the humbled submissive slave that believed God put him in chains. A question he repeatedly posed in his messages was: "Could a slave owner be a true Christian?"

His speaking itinerary grew; he traveled and spoke in many places. In Britain in 1846, he gave a speech in London's Finsbury Chapel hosted by the British and Foreign Anti-Slavery Society. His fiery words spoke about the deep, sinister hypocrisy of the Southern clergy. The fiery message spoke right to the core of the blatant evil in the churches. According to Dilbeck:

> Douglass began his speech with describing the horrors of slavery. With the weight of a prophetic mantel he spoke: Master denied their slaves the chance to receive an education, to marry, or even to read the Bible. No weapon was too cruel for slaveholders to enforce their reign: Starvation, the bloody whip, the chain, the gag, the thumb-screw, among others. This cruelty was the plight of American slaves, Douglass told his listeners, the millions in bondage who lived and suffered in a nation "boasting of its liberty, boasting of its humanity, boasting of its Christianity, boasting of its love of justice and purity."[85]

For the rest of his speech at Finsbury Chapel, Douglass dwelt on the tragic disconnect between the boasts of Christian America and the fate of its slaves. Here he spoke in full prophetic form. Southern religion remained "the great supporter, the great sanctioner" of all the "bloody atrocities" American slaves endured. Support for slavey had become an essential pillar of Christian orthodoxy as practiced in the white south, Douglass said. Ministers of Christ's gospel were the most ardent defenders of the institution. Each Sunday, they stood in the pulpit and lent their support to slavery, delivering sermons that "torture the hallowed pages of inspired wisdom." Douglass concluded that the "darkest feature of slavery" was the unequivocal support it received from the white southern clergy, which exposed any critic of the institution to "the charge of infidelity." The ultimate irony of proslavery Christianity was that it labeled slavery's opponents heretic and its supporters orthodox.[86]

Douglas assured his British audiences that he never wavered in his faithfulness to the Christianity of Christ, rightly understood. "I love it,' he told an audience in Cork, Ireland, October 1845. "I love that religion which is from above, without partiality or hypocrisy—that religion based upon that broad, that world—embracing principle, 'That whatever you would that men should do to you, do ye even so to them.' Douglass forever found in the gospel of Christ a powerful weapon against southern proslavery religion.[87]

Douglass was a true prophet of God. Prophets in the Bible varied in their roles. In the Old Testament, most were governmental and spoke, admonished, and warned of coming judgments and disasters if God's people did not repent. God sent many to expose wickedness and rot that settled in the heart of his people. Miracles, signs, and wonders were brought through their hands in many instances. Prophets could clearly see the division and idolatry that came from rebellion and greed.

Douglass was raised out of the ash heap to speak and warn of the upcoming judgement if the church did not repent of her sin of slavery.

*If my people, which are called by my name, shall humble themselves, and pray, and seek my face, and turn from their wicked ways; then will I hear from heaven, and will forgive their sin, and will heal their land.*

2 Chronicles 7:14 (KVJ)

God's people are always the key to changing the direction of a nation if that nation humbles itself and prays. The South was deceived and full of greed. They thought they were doing God's will and receiving his blessing. In the case of the South during Douglass's times, riches were deceitful; the abundance was not God's blessing but the work of extortion, pride, and greed. The love of money is the root of ALL evil. They loved their money. They were blind to the hate, murder, and cruelty required to obtain their money.

Douglass could see it clearly and he spoke against it all his life. He warned them that God will judge that wicked institution of slavery. That judgment came through the Civil War.

When the Civil War began, Douglass knew God's hand was in it to destroy the power of slavery in the United States. During the war, he continued to speak and exhort his fellow abolitionists. He became a national leader and used his gifts to continue fighting for freedom, mercy, and justice. He lived through transformational changes in the United States. He lived to witness the Civil War and fought for the 13th Amendment, that which legally forbade slavery in the United States and freed all slaves without compensation to slave owners.

He also witnessed the passing of the 14th and 15th Amendments. The 14th declared all persons born or naturalized in the United States were entitled to equal rights regardless of their race, and that their rights were protected at both the state and national levels. The 15th declared that citizens could not be denied the right to vote because of race, color or previous condition of servitude. These amendments passed between 1865-1870. Douglass witnessed the miraculous. These amendments—occurring within five years—transformed the nation. He believed God was a good father and he saw his vision come to pass. Of course, those amendments didn't solve the problem of the deep-rooted racism cultivated in the nation, but they were foundational breakthroughs comparable to the parting of the Red Sea.

Douglass never wavered in the foundation of his faith that God was good and slavery was evil. He experienced that goodness and led many people in the same beliefs.

> *I had fainted, unless I had believed to see the goodness of*
> *the LORD in the land of the living.*
>
> Psalm 23:7 (KJV)

Douglass never wavered or fainted but stood firm, and God rewarded him.

# 31

# Bonhoeffer

THE RELATIONSHIP BETWEEN CHURCH AND GOVERNMENT has changed throughout history. When studying the life of Bonhoeffer, we see how Acts 5:29, "We must obey God rather than men," was applied during Hitler's reign and the Nazi regime.

In the 1930s, Dietrich Bonhoeffer studied at Union Theological Seminary and became interested in racial injustice. These studies laid the foundation for his return to Germany years later. When he returned to Germany, his relationship with the Lord deepened, and he began understanding his calling to the Church. That calling took on a depth and seriousness in his lectures and teachings. His messages were about waking up the Church from playing Church and becoming true disciples of Jesus. In the years preceding the rise of Hitler, Bonhoeffer sensed the dark days ahead for the German Church. He did his best to prepare the Church through lectures and sermons.

Then in 1933, Hitler became the Chancellor of Germany and the Third Reich was established. Bonhoeffer, his family, and many others saw right through Hitler. From the beginning of Hitler's reign, Bonhoeffer preached against it. The law of Nazi Germany required citizens to obey Hitler, yet Bonhoeffer refused to take the oath. Nazi flags were put up in churches and Bonhoeffer tore them down. As a result, he was banned from teaching and preaching, but that didn't stop him.

The dark reign came down hard on the German Evangelical Church. With the influence of National Socialism, the Church became divided as many Protestant leaders and church members embraced the rise of Nazism. A group called Deutsch Christen, which is translated "German Christians" actively encouraged the Nazification of German

Protestantism, thus forming a pro-Nazi church. It would become the "Reich Church." These German Christians wanted to implement "Aryan laws" in their new churches. They became outspoken and antagonistic toward those who didn't agree with them. This caused division and confusion in the Christian Community.

According to Holocaust Encyclopedia;

> In the early years following Hitler's appointment as Chancellor in 1933, the term Aryan was used in various areas of public life in Nazi Germany, including in legislation. The first major law to revoke the rights of Jewish citizens was the "Law for the Restoration of the Professional Civil Service." Issued on April 7, 1933, the Civil Service Law included a clause referred to as the Arie paragraph (Aryan Paragraph). This was the first legal formulation used to exclude Jews (and often by extension other "non-Aryans") from organizations, professions, and other aspects of public life. As the law stated, "Civil servants who are not of Aryan descent are to be retired." Other organizations, including private or religious ones, followed suit, introducing an Aryan clause for membership.[88]

Even though antisemitism grew with enthusiasm, most church leaders opposed the Aryan paragraph initially, but as time passed, the debate confused many church leaders. This confusion astounded Bonhoeffer because he knew the Aryan paragraph was steeped in racism. But eventually, the Pro-Nazi Christians gained control of the German Evangelical Church—the country's largest Protestant Church. Those Churches became an arm of the Nazi Party.

The deep oppression that settled on the Church brought forth another group of Christians that opposed Nazi rule. They resisted the premise that Christ, as the head of the Church, could be replaced by an earthly ruler or governing authority. Christ was the supreme ruler over the Church and Christians. This new Church called itself the

Confessing Church. Bonhoeffer became one of the strongest leaders of the Confessing Church. Because of persecution, the Confessing Church was forced to go underground. Still, many members, including leaders, stayed silent about the persecution of the Jews, and most church leaders refused to oppose the Nazi regime openly. Those leaders also berated their fellow leaders and associates who did speak out. This caused division in the Confessing Church between those relentless in their convictions and those trying to stay safe. The Confessing Christians were at war from all sides.

Bonhoeffer served as pastor to several German-speaking congregations in London from September 1933 to April 1935. He led them to break with the official German Church and join the Confessing Church. In April 1935, Bonhoeffer returned to Germany, where the Confessing Church was under increasing pressure from the Gestapo. He trained young ministers at an illegal Confessing Church seminary. The seminary, called Finkenwalde was closed down by the Gestapo, and Bonhoeffer went underground, operating throughout eastern Germany to mentor his students, many of whom were working illegally in small congregations.

**Resistance Activities**

Bonhoeffer's brother-in-law, Hans von Dohanyi, worked in the Justice Ministry and opposed the Nazi regime. Bonhoeffer was kept informed about different German resistance plans. His brother-in-law helped him avoid military service by obtaining an assignment for him in the office of Military Intelligence. Bonhoeffer made several trips outside the Nazi regime as an informant for the Military Intelligence office. He used his connections with Hans to help Confessing pastors evade military service and became involved in rescuing Jews from Germany.

Bonhoeffer was eventually arrested and charged with conspiring to rescue Jews, and the Gestapo uncovered his other resistance work. In February 1945, he was moved to Buchenwald concentration camp, and in April, to the Flossenburg concentration camp. On April 9, 1945, the Nazis hung him with other conspirators. His brother, Klaus Bonhoeffer, and his brothers-in-law Hans and Rüdiger Schleicher were also executed.

Romans 13 tells us that civil servants are servants of God, and that civil servants were placed in authority to do good, punish evil-doers, and reward the just. But what happens when the rulers become evil?

During the time of Hitler, confusion and division set in the Church because of fear. No sane human being wants to be executed. If there was an escape, anyone would take it. The fear of death drove many to stay silent. God rose up those he chose to speak out against evil and stand. Bonhoeffer and his associates stood against pure evil. They paid the ultimate price, yet the atrocities against humankind were too horrific for these martyrs to ignore.

Wisdom weighs and discerns all things. Christ has given us wisdom from heaven. During Hitler's reign, nationalism became fascism, which became Nazism. The Nazis wanted supreme rulership even over Christ himself. The Antichrist had risen its head in full color during that time.

Ultimately, God will judge each human being according to their works and conscience. Bonhoeffer's conscience could not allow him to be silent. Like many in the first-century Church, he resisted the authorities and sacrificed his life for the lives of many.

# 32

# Civil Rights

THE CIVIL RIGHTS MOVEMENT would have never come into being without the Church rising to oppose the injustices that prevailed against the black community. In fact, according to Paul Harvey:

> It is impossible to conceive of the civil rights movement without placing black Christianity at its center, for it empowered the rank and file who made the movement move. And when it moved, it demolished the system of legal segregation.[89]

Christians were the movers and shakers of the civil rights movement, but there was a stark division in the churches between those who caught the fire and those who stood on the sidelines and watched the cultural divide burn.

Black and white Christian activists worked tirelessly to abolish the Jim Crow laws and the blatant racism and injustices that happened regularly. Yet other Christians, both black and white, stayed out of the fray completely. Many church leaders refused to get involved in the movement. There were several reasons for this. In his book, *Freedom's Coming*, Paul Harvey writes:

> It is sometimes said that the civil rights movement emerged from "the black church" a falsely singular term for what was in fact a multifarious set of institutions. Historians cite evidence such as churches that served as gathering points for mass meetings. For the black Southerner, the Church was the center of cultural life. But activists also contended with the reality that "the black church" was not, as a rule, behind the movement. Because of indifference, fear, theological

conservatism, or coercion and terrorism, many congregations simply avoided involvement.[90]

There was, of course, good reason for the fear. In the early summer of 1964, forty-one black churches in Mississippi of various denominations went up in flames. The tragedy of this is the terror it instilled in many people, yet with others there arose a passion to fight. Those with more to lose stayed out of the fight as much as possible. According to Harvey:

> A white student stationed in southwest Georgia in 1965 tellingly concluded that the movement was "saturated with religion," but for him the "most shocking discovery… was to find how conservative and separate from the movement are most Negro churches." He generally found religious leaders "far more conservative than the people in many cases." Black churches were a "very active" stumbling block, another activist observed, often still beholden to a theology "based on a heaven-centered world view coupled with a demeaning view of the power of man. These two tenets fulfill the function of keeping the Negro in his place." White churches, too, refused "to take any meaningful step in the direction of integration," with most clergy unwilling to "allow any type of integrated meeting within their sacred walls." Ministers who shied away from involvement were not necessarily opposed to the movement but might have been "just afraid to join it openly. It's simply a contradiction: so many preachers support the movement that we can say it was based in churches, yet many preachers couldn't take sides with it because they thought they had too much to lose.[91]

This quote seems to contradict the notion that black Christianity was at the center of the Civil Rights movement. The fact is, Black Christianity was at the center, not necessarily Black religious institutions. Again, as in the past, God raised up his Christian warriors to fight the cultural and civil wars. While the religious institutions became the stumbling block for new movements and shakings worldwide, the Christian cultural warriors became the backbone of the movement.

One such warrior was a peaceful soldier named Martin Luther King Jr. He established the Southern Christian Leadership Conference (SCLC) with the vision of redeeming "the soul of America." He gathered and organized Black churches to support the SCLC. His method was nonviolent resistance. King wrote, with fellow ministers C.K. Steele and Fred Shuttlesworth, "because we have no moral choice, before God, but to delve deeper into the struggle—and to do so with greater reliance on non-violence and with greater unity, coordination, sharing with Christian understanding."

SCLC staff trained local communities in the philosophy of Christian nonviolence by conducting leadership training programs and opening citizenship schools. Through its affiliation with churches and its advocacy of nonviolence, SCLC sought to frame the struggle for civil rights in moral terms. The SCLC's leadership, most of whom were ministers, also believed that churches should be involved in political activism. They held many of their meetings at Black churches, which became important symbols in the battle for civil rights.[92]

One of the churches, the Sixteenth Street Baptist Church, became heavily involved in marches and demonstrations in Birmingham, Alabama. Many of the marchers were schoolchildren. Thousands came out in support of ending segregation in Birmingham. This support brought civil unrest as it was aired on TV and viewed by millions all over the world. These Christians were strong, courageous, and full of faith. In September 1963, a bomb exploded in the church, killing four young girls attending Sunday School. It also injured more than 20 other members of the church. This murderous act brought worldwide awareness of racism in the nation.

Citizenship schools were another outreach of SCLC. They helped establish 900 schools in rural areas throughout the South. These schools helped African Americans pass literacy tests required for voter registration. They also trained people to become community activists. The teachers—typically taught by local women with economic resources, community networks, and connection to local groups— discussed and instructed how to effect change locally-defined problems. Through these classes, students learned more than literacy; they synthesized their own understanding of American citizenship.

Citizenship schools became the core component for all the organizations involved in the Civil Rights Movement.

Here is an example of a class schedule:

### SCLC Citizenship Education Program (Mississippi)

Programs trains local housewives, ministers, retired teachers, beauticians, farmers, tradesmen, seamstresses, others who read and write legibly and are interested in aiding in the struggle to gain first class citizenship and will help other to do so. These persons must be willing to give tow night a week for 12 weeks to teach a class in basic citizenship.

The Citizenship Program operates in 12 counties:

| | | | |
|---|---|---|---|
| LEFLORE | SUNFLOWER | MADISON | FORREST |
| BOLIVAR | WASHINGTON | LSAKE | HOLMES |
| COAHOMA | HINDS | LAUDERDALE | OKTIBEHA |

The program may be divided into two parts:

#### CLASSROOM ACTIVITIES
1. Literacy; voter registration
2. Negro history (past and current)
3. Government; American history
4. Freedom Movement
5. Nonviolence
6. Citizenship rights and responsibilities
7. Conducting business- using a bank, writing money orders, applications, telegrams, income tax forms
8. Current events
9. Speakers, films, trips, outings, etc.

#### COMMUNITY (COFO) ACTIVITIES
Voter registration (canvassing, etc
Freedom day protests (Greenwood, Hattiesburg, etc.)
Poll tax drives
cooperate with NAACP and other civic groups
COFO Staff and State-wide Meetings
COFO Welfare and Relief Committees
  Block captains
  Citizenship clubs

COFO Summer Project:
1. provide and locate housing
2. recruit students for freedom schools
3. serve as deputy registrars
4. raising funds for "Freedom Campaigns"
(Freedom Party)

#### POLICIES:
1. Training people to work in their own communities; to take active role in gaining freedoms; to make decisions on their own. To learn to be leaders. Persons must attend Dorchester workshop.
2. Teachers work voluntarily. SCLC provide 30 a month for operational expense ( fuel, electricity, transportation and other costs incidental to the work) supervisors also receive operational expense.
3. CEP staff are asked to inform Greenwood and/or Atlanta office of SCLC before engaging in any activity which may be known or expected to lead to arrest. (This is necessary in order to ascertain bond available and/or make plans to raise bond money.)

\*\*\*\*\*\*\*\*\*\*\*\*\*\*\*\*\*\*\*\*\*\*\*\*\*\*\*\*\*\*\*\*\*\*\*\*\*\*\*\*\*\*\*\*\*\*\*\*\*\*\*\*\*\*\*\*\*\*\*\*\*\*\*\*\*

The citizenship classes offered to teach local ministers, in the hope that the ministers would teach their congregations. Christians were the leaders of the movement.

Here are some paragraphs from Martin Luther King Jr.'s speech at a Baptist Church in Albany.

> And I want to ask about another group because I'm intimately associated with it. I want to know where the Christian people, who go to church every Sunday morning, stand. I want to hear from them (Yes, Amen), for you see, it may well be that we will have to repent in this generation not merely from the loud and bitter words of the bad people but for the appalling silence of the good people.

> This disturbs me and I believe it disturbs you. It disturbs me to see ministers of the gospel laymen, trying to go to worship in churches in Albany, and they can't worship. A Methodist minister, Reverend Ralph Roy from New York City, went to his own denomination with a Negro. And do you know they turned him back? Oh, how tragic this is. (It's tragic, Yes, Well, Right) Eleven o'clock on Sunday morning, when we stand to sing "In Christ There Is No East or West," is the most segregated hour in America, and the Sunday school is the most segregated school of the week. How tragic this is.

> To use Dr. Anderson terms, Dr. Anderson's terms that he would use as a doctor, too often in the church and particularly the white church, we have a high blood pressure of creeds and an anemia of deeds. It's time now (Amen) that we begin to shake the lethargy from our souls. We are going to be children of the almighty God. If our white brothers are going to be Christians, they must go on back to the Old Testament (That's right), hear Amos crying out, "Let justice roll down (Yes) like water and righteousness like a mighty stream." They must go on over and turn till they get to Micah, hear

him as he cries out in words that echo across the centuries: "What doth the Lord require of thee (Yes, Yes), but to do justly, to love mercy (Yes), and to walk humbly with thy God." Go with me, if you will, on over to the New Testament. Stand with Paul as he stands on Mars Hill and cries out, "Out of one blood God made all men to dwell upon the face of the earth." Then stand with me. Watch our Lord and master as he moves around the Galilean hills. Hear him as he said, "Blessed are the pure in heart for they shall see God. Blessed are the meek, for they shall inherit the earth. Do unto others as you would have them do unto you." Our white brothers in Albany need to hear these words. That's the second point I want to bring out.

The third point I want to bring out is something that I've been wanting to say to you, because something can be said to you so long that you come to believe it. I reread a book a few weeks ago written by a man named Adolph Hitler—you've heard of him. It's a book called Mein Kampf; he says in that book, among other things, that if you are going to tell a lie—and he implies that to be a good dictator you have to do it—he says tell a big lie. And if you tell it long and loud enough, everybody will soon believe it, even yourself. So now, we've been hearing a lot of things, and I'm afraid that we're going to come to believe these things if we don't straighten them out. [93]

Christianity was at the center of the Civil Rights Movement. God was in it because he is not only a father but a judge—a judge who judges righteously. The fire for civil rights was the fire of God. Some people had wicked agendas and led astray many. That caused deep roots of bitterness and hatred. But God's will for justice still prevailed. King and the leadership in the SCLC brought awareness of the prevalence of racism and initiated the foundation for the passage of the Civil Rights Act of 1964 and the Voting Rights Act of 1965.

With God, nothing is impossible in this world.

# 33

# The Pro-Life Movement

THE PRO-LIFE MOVEMENT started in the 1930s among those who spoke against abortion. The first right-to-life organizations created in the mid-1960s were Catholic. The Pro-life movement evolved over the years from Catholic doctors, bishops, and lawyers, and were mostly Democrats. Now, the Pro-Life movement is a combination of Conservative Catholics and Protestants that are mostly Republicans. What happened?

In the 1930s, the pro-life movement encompassed more than stopping abortion, and the pro-choice movement was not about abortion on demand. According to Daniel K. Williams, in *Defenders of the Unborn*:

> The pro-life movement thought of itself from the very beginning not as a movement primarily devoted to opposing abortion-though that is what it essentially became-but as a movement to defend the legal protection of all human life from the moment of conception. Pro-lifers saw themselves as defenders of the "inalienable and legally enshrined in the Fifth and Fourteenth Amendments of the Constitution. They argued that this right to life began at the moment of conception. Their opponents accused them of campaigning against abortion primarily because of their religious views or discomfort with women's rights, but pro-lifers rejected those accusations. They defended the value of all human life, as outlined in the nation's founding documents. Thus, in their view, the term "Prolife" was the most accurate descriptor of their political project.

In the early years, before the 1960s, the pro-choice movement was about preventing the birth of unwanted children (particularly if they were likely to be born with severe deformities), reducing population growth, and giving doctors greater legal protections in making choices that they thought would be in the best interests of their patients. In its early years, the campaign for legalizing abortion was a medical or population control movement, not a women's rights cause." [94]

Before Roe, the Catholic Church combined birth control and abortion. Catholics lumped birth control, sterilization, and abortion together as disobeying God's commandment to fill the earth, and they felt all three procedures were an attack on human life. Protestants took a different view. They believed birth control was an acceptable social norm and helped families benefit economically and socially. On the issue of abortion, they thought it was the taking of human life and should only be done in extreme circumstances. In fact, according to Williams, "No Protestant denomination passed an official resolution on abortion till the 1960s. During their silence, the pro-choice movement grew and expanded." (Williams pg. 28)

The Catholics were alone in their fight until Roe V. Wade. Most pro-life Catholics were Democrats because they believed in many of that party's social policies, including individual rights, minority rights, ministry to the poor and afflicted, workers' rights, and a living wage. To the Catholics, this was all-inclusive to human life and rights.

The Catholic bishops had tight control over their Catholic legislators until the pro-choice movement expanded from a population control movement and eugenics to a women's right to choose over her body. In the past, bishops and priests could sway their parishioners on how to vote. But as the pro-choice movement became a women's rights movement, the Catholic hierarchy lost power in the legislature. One famous Catholic family, the Kennedys, eventually turned on their pro-life stance. Ted Kennedy was an advocate for the pro-life movement until the 1970s. He remained steadfast in his personal view against abortion, but he refused to support pro-life bills in Congress. Many Catholic legislators turned on the pro-life movement when they saw that the Catholic leadership had lost its influence on their churches.

The Catholic Church could not turn to the Republicans at that time either. The Republican party was the party of Protestants and businesses, and they had no interest in getting involved in the pro-life movement. President Ford was not against abortion; his wife, Betty, was a strong supporter and declared that Roe was a great decision. Ford's Vice President was Nelson Rockefeller. In 1966, he was New York's governor and called for "abortion reform."

President Richard Nixon signed a bill to create a Commission on Population Growth and the American Future in March 1970, something he had promised to do a year earlier. The chairman of the Commission was New York's Republican Governor Nelson Rockefeller, about whom Nixon observed: "Perhaps no person in the world has been more closely or longer identified with this problem." The Rockefeller Foundation, along with the Ford Foundation, had funded many of the studies. Rockefeller's grandmother, Abby Rockefeller, was one of Margaret Sanger's best friends and her largest donor. One Rockefeller-funded initiative was the development of the American Law Institute's Model Penal Code, through which abortion laws were loosened, state by state, based on sex studies by the Kinsey Institute.[95]

Ronald Reagan, as governor of California, signed an abortion liberalization bill in 1967, and the strongest influence on him, Nancy Reagan, was actively hostile to pro-life. "I don't give a damn about the right-to-lifers," Nancy retorted as she edited pro-life language out of her husband's state of the Union speech one year. [96]

Population control and eugenics were a vast topic; much of it was funded and driven by wealthy Republicans who controlled the Republican Party at the time. The Republican party fully supported and endorsed abortion.

Historically, the Democratic Party has been the Catholic Party and the Republican Party the Protestant Party. How did the pro-life movement get on the Republican platform?

According to George McKenna:

> The Democratic Party and the Catholic Church have always been on the same wavelength as regards social and economic rights, particularly the rights of the poor, weak, and vulnerable members of society. The great majority of Catholic clergy were Democrats. Born in working-class homes, they attended Catholic schools and were usually the first generation to get a higher education—mainly in Catholic colleges and seminaries. Even the least reflective among them could see that the social teaching they absorbed in those colleges was strikingly similar to the domestic platform of the Democratic Party.[97]

The Republican Party was born in a Congregational church in Ripon, Wisconsin, in 1854. Many of its members were Protestants who emerged from the Puritans. Young people became activists during Civil Rights Movement, and this continued during the Vietnam War. This movement included Catholics with Secular Humanists. The anti-war movement brought liberalism to the forefront, knocking out the traditional Catholic Democrat in government. By 1975, the Democratic Party became the party not only of social welfare and business regulation but of many other causes:

- environmentalism
- consumer protection
- affirmative action
- gun control
- arms control
- multilateralism
- rapprochement with the Soviets
- the Equal Rights Amendment.

The Catholic bishops were not interested in all of these issues. So, their Democrat legislators turned away from bishops and endorsed a more liberal platform. Catholics were torn because they believed in human and worker's rights, not big business. The Catholic Church was divided into parts—the young liberals of the 60s and the traditionalists of the 40s and 50s. This division weakened the Church and caused its voice in pro-life causes to diminish.

Eventually, the Republican party found that supporting life would benefit the party. Ronald Reagan led that cause and pulled Conservative Democrats from the party to vote for him. In the Republican Party, there is still division on how much attention should be given to the abortion issue. Republicans also still divide between the fiscal moderates and the social conservatives.

The Roe v. Wade decision brought the Protestants a huge wake-up call. Conservative Protestants and Catholics joined together, and the conservative Christians rose to fight for the rights of the unborn. Institutional religion and churches split on abortion, and the institutional church did little to organize or speak up against it. The topic of abortion was, and still is, one of the most polarizing subjects that church leaders avoid discussing. It was the pro-life organizations outside the Catholic and Protestant churches that entered the frontlines of the battle. These organizations were from Catholic and Protestant people.

Here are some of the major contributors to this cause:

- National Right to Life, founded in 1968, is the nation's oldest and largest pro-life organization. National Right to Life is the federation of 50 state right-to-life affiliates and more than 3,000 local chapters. Through education and legislation, National Right to Life is working to restore legal protection to the most defenseless members of our society who are threatened by abortion, infanticide, assisted suicide, and euthanasia.

- The Christian Coalition of America is committed to representing the pro-family agenda and educating Americans on our society's critical issues. Whether it is the fight to end Partial Birth Abortion or efforts to improve education, or lower the family's tax burden,
- Priests for Life is a particular effort to galvanize the clergy to preach, teach, and mobilize their people more effectively to end abortion and euthanasia.
- Students For Life Of America has grown up to become one of the leading pro-life advocacy organizations in the world.

In 2022, Roe v. Wade was overturned by the committed Christians that refused to accept the doctrine of death. Christians joined together to fight for human life. The pro-life movement is a civil rights movement that will continue till our Lord returns.

# Conclusion

IN MAKING THE CASE for why the Church should be in government, I'm not suggesting that the Church should look to government to solve all its problems or answer its prayers. The governments of this world are not the Kingdom of God. We live in the world but are not of this world, yet we are commanded to go into the world.

> *They are not of the world, just as I am not of the world.*
>
> John 17:16 (ESV)

> *And he [Jesus] said to them, "Go into all the world and proclaim the gospel to the whole creation."*
>
> Mark 16:15 (ESV)

To fully understand the purpose of government, the church needs wisdom from God and knowledge from his Word. Could it be that earthly government positions are a training ground for ruling and reigning with Christ for all eternity? Perhaps the stakes are higher than we suppose.

Instead of avoiding the political process, let's engage it. Jesus' command: "Go into all the world," doesn't just mean standing behind a pulpit or taking your family to a third-world nation. There are many ways to impart the gospel of Christ to humanity. Ministry is sacrifice. It involves reaching out and giving of ourselves for Christ and his kingdom. Christians must participate in government as if it was a ministerial calling. Governmental service is a place where God can use a person to orchestrate great change and fulfill his divine plan for his people. It is a place where history is made. It is an institution through which God can use the church to change the world.

I am concluding this book with a powerful and persuasive statement from Fr. Frank Pavone:

The Church does not have a political mission, she nevertheless has a political responsibility to bear witness to those moral truths without which the common good—which is the very purpose for which governments are instituted—cannot survive. These moral truths are basic and go beyond the bounds of any denominational beliefs. Because they are truths, they must shape public policy. Not only do individuals have a duty to obey God, but so do governments. Moreover, the people of God do not lose their citizenship on earth by virtue of the fact that they are citizens of heaven (see Philippians 3:20). If anything, our belief in heaven makes us more concerned about the earth, not less concerned. Why? Because the good that we bring about on earth is not lost in the next world but remains and grows. Human life and activity continue in the world to come, which is why they are so important to us now. Christians have a duty to be politically active, to register and vote, to lobby and educate candidates and elected officials, and to speak up about the issues that Conclusion affect the common good. Now is the time, now is the challenge. No longer are we to think of our religion as a purely "private matter." Christ taught in public, and he was crucified in public. Now risen from the dead, he places us in the public arena, with the commission to make disciples of all nations (see Matthew 28:18-20). May we not fail him or our nation.[98]

# About The Author

MARY SALAMON IS PASSIONATE about Government and the Church merging to change regions and nations. The church is to equip and mobilize the body of Christ for effective service in taking the Gospel to the world and redeeming the world around us, including the prophetic role of assuring accountability in government to God's standards. The State/government is to protect the innocent's life, property, and freedom and punish those violating those rights. Mary's writings unite people from both institutions to understand each other's roles better. She served as the Washington State Leader for the Governor's Prayer Team and currently participates in local, state, and national government. She loves her God, family, and country. She resides in the Pacific Northwest and is the mother of three grown sons and eight wonderful grandchildren. She is available for church, conference, and civic event speaking engagements.

Contact Mary:
https://www.godgovernmentandgoodness.com/home
Subscribe to her Substack:
https://marysalamon.substack.com/

# Bibliography

Ackerman, Susan. Warrior, Dancer, Seductress, Queen: Women in Judges and Biblical Israel. New York: Doubleday, 1998.

Aling, Charles F. Egypt and Bible History: From Earliest Times to 1000 B.C. Grand Rapids, Michigan: Baker, 1981.

Aristotle. Politics. Sage Publications, Inc., 2006.

Baldwin, Joyce G. Daniel. Downers Grove, Illinois: IVP Academic, 1978.

Barton, David. Founders Bible. Greenville: Shiloh Road, 2014. Print.

Boice, James Montgomery. Nehemiah. Grand Rapids, Michigan: Baker, 2005.

Boyd, Gregory A. God of the Possible: A Biblical Introduction to the Open View of God. Gale, Cengage Learning, 2000.

Catt, Carrie Chapman and Nettie Rogers Shuler. Woman Suffrage and Politics. 1923.

Clifford-Larson, Kate. Bound for the Promised Land. New York: Ballantine. 2003.

Cundall and Morris. Judges and Ruth. Downers Grove, Illinois: Tyndale, 1968.

Dilbeck, D.H. Frederick Douglass-America's Prophet. Chapel Hill. 2018.

Finkelstein, Israel, and Neil Asher Silberman. The Bible Unearthed: Archaeology's New Vision of 138 Ancient Israel and the Origin of Its Sacred Texts. New York: Touchstone, 2002.

Harvey, Paul. Freedom's Coming. North Carolina: North Carolina Press, 2005.

Julian Spriggs, Peter and Paul and the Authority of the Citizen

Lambert, W.G. Babylonian Wisdom Literature. Oxford, 1960. Patton, George S. and George S. Patton Jr. War as I Knew It. Boston: Houghton Mifflin Co., 1995.

O'Reilly, Bill. Killing Jesus. New York, Holt, 2013. Print.

Prince, Derek. Praying for the Government. Derek Prince Ministries, 2012. Kindle edition.

Putnam, Robert. Bowling Alone: The Collapse and Revival of American Community. New York: Simon and Shuster, 2000.

Paine, Thomas. Thomas Paine: Collected Writings. New York, New York: The Library of America, 1995.

Reynolds, David. Mightier Than the Sword. New York: Norton. 2011.

Robertson, Pat, and Bob Slosser. The Secret Kingdom. Nashville, Tennessee: W Publishing Group, 1992.

Saia, Michael. Why Pray? Edmonds, Washington, 2014.

Sire, James W. The Universe Next Door: A Basic Worldview Catalog. Intervarsity Press, 2009. E-book.

The Framing of a Right to Choose: Roe v Wade and the Changing Debate on abortion Law," Law and History Review 27, 2009

Weinfeld, Moshe, and S. Sperling. Deuteronomy. Gale, 2007. E-book.

Westbrook, Raymond, and Bruce Wells. Everyday Law in Biblical Israel: An Introduction. Louisville, Kentucky: Westminster John Knox, 2009.

Yamauchi, Edwin M. Persia and the Bible. Grand Rapids, Michigan Baker, 1990.

# Endnotes

[1] Robert Putnam, Bowling Alone, 42.

[2] Sire, The Universe Next Door, 20.

[3] Paine, Thomas Paine: Collected Writings, 13.

[4] Boyd, God of the Possible, page 102.

[5] Dictionary.com, s.v. "occupy."

[6] Strong's Handi-Reference Concordance, s.v. "thrones," "dominion," and "power."

[7] Robertson and Slosser, The Secret Kingdom, 199.

[8] http://www.biblearchaeology.org/post/2010/02/23/Joseph-in-Egypt-Part-II.aspx.

[9] http://www.biblearchaeology.org/post/2010/02/23/Joseph-in-Egypt-Part-II.aspx

[10] http://www.biblearchaeology.org/post/2010/03/04/Joseph-in-Egypt-Part-III.aspx.

[11] Ibid

[12] http://www.biblearchaeology.org/post/2010/04/05/Joseph-in-Egypt-Part-V.aspx.

[13] Ibid.d

[14] Aling, Egypt and Bible History, 74.

[15] Westbrook and Wells, Everyday Law, 22-23.

[16] Ibid., 22-24.

[17] https://en.wikipedia.org/wiki/Code_of_Hammurabi.

[18] Cundall and Morris, Judges and Ruth, 136

[19] Ackerman, Warrior, Dancer, Seductress, Queen, 29 and 42-43.

[20] Oxford English Dictionary, s.v. "just."

21 Dictionary.com, s.v. "covet."

22 Finkelstein and Silberman, The Bible Unearthed, 181-182.

23 Quoted in Lambert, Babylonian Wisdom Literature, 3-4.

24 https://www.gotquestions.org/Gad-in-the-Bible.html

25 https://www.gotquestions.org/Nathan-in-the-Bible.html

26 Quoted in Lambert, Babylonian Wisdom Literature, 3-4.

27 Baldwin, Daniel, 92.

28 http://jbq.jewishbible.org/assets/Uploads/6/jbq_6_3_final.pdf, 115-117

29 Boice, Nehemiah, 126-128.

30 http://www.gospelpolitics.com/jesus-and-politics.html

31 O'Reilly, Bill. Killing Jesus. New York, Holt, 2013. Print.

32 Ibid.

33 http://ntwrightpage.com/Wright_Paul_Caesar_Romans.htm.

34 Julian Spriggs, Peter and Paul and the Authority of the Citizen

35 O'Reilly, Bill. Killing Jesus. New York, Holt, 2013. Print.

36 Hanson-Davis, Victor. The Dying Citizen. New York: Hatchet,2021. Print

37 Weinfeld, Moshe, and S. Sperling. Deuteronomy. Gale, 2007. E-book.

38 Patton and Patton Jr., War as I Knew It. Sanage Publishing House; 1st edition, August 12, 2020. Print.

39 Ibid.

40 Saia, Michael, Why Pray?, Xulon Press March 27, 2014. Pages 31, 36, 38, 41.

41 Prince, Derek. Praying for the Government. Derek Prince Ministries, 2012. Kindle edition.

42 https://www.ifapray.org/resources/prayer-guides-and- resources/.

43 Catt, Champman and Shuler, Woman Suffrage and Politics.

44 https://ballotpedia.org/All-mail_voting#Debate

45 https://tuesdayshorse.wordpress.com/2009/01/13/horses- have-a-hero-in-new-yorks-tedisco-us/.

46 https://dailygazette.com/article/2009/12/19/1220_buster.

47 https://www.thepetitionsite.com/petition/.

48 https://www.thepetitionsite.com/cause-to-successful- petition/.

49 From the notes of a Family Policy Institute workshop called Olympia 301.

50 http://www.goodhousekeeping.com/life/parenting/a39575/my-neighbor-saved-my-sons-life.

51 Bethune, "The End of Neighbors." https://www.macleans.ca/ society/the-end-of-neighbours/.

52 https://www.blueletterbible.org//lang/lexicon/lexicon. Strongs=G4139&t=NKJV.

53 http://www.denverdweller.com/neighborhood-community- reads/.

54 https://www.forbes.com/sites/steveforbes/2011/09/09/ remembering-911-the-rudy-giuliani-interview/#1c18e0503a7d

55 https://www.commentarymagazine.com/culture-civilization/ history/giuliani-leadership-on-911/.

56 https://wacities.org/docs/default-source/ resources/mayorscouncilmembershandbookwebec 4f3b49b78160ed9eadff0000bbe4eb.pdf?sfvrsn=0

57 https://work.chron.com/role-police-officer-8056.html.

58 https://firstliberty.org/.

59 https://firstliberty.org/cases/.

60 http://capta6.org/docs/whatdoesthePTAdo.pdf.

61 http://www.steelecanyonathleticboosters.com/ uploads/1/3/3/3/13337542/schs_boosters_membership_generic. pdf.

62 http://www.colorincolorado.org/article/parent-participation- how-get-involved-your-childs-school-activities.

63 https://thefederalist.com/2021/06/21/moms-must-keep-hammering-school-boards-until-critical-race-theory-is-dead/

[64] https://aflegal.org/guides/

[65] Aristotle. Politics. Sage Publications, Inc., 2006.

[66] https://www.opendoorsusa.org/christian-persecution/world- watch-list/about-the-ranking/ and https://www.opendoorsusa. org/christian-persecution/stories/5-gut-wrenching-facts-north- korean-prison-camps/.

[67] https://diplomacy.state.gov/discoverdiplomacy/ diplomacy101/people/170341.htm.

[68] https://en.wikipedia.org/wiki/J._Christopher_Stevens

[69] Barton, David. Founders Bible. Greenville: Shiloh Road, 2014. Print.

[70] https://www.au.org/wp-content/uploads/migration/pdf_documents/JeffersonDanburyBaptists.pdf

[71] http://www.emersonkent.com/speeches/abolition.htm

[72] https://www.christianitytoday.com/history/issues/issue-2/wesley-to-wilberforce.html

[73] https://www.cslewisinstitute.org/wp-content/uploads/KD-2001-Summer-William-Wilberforce-and-His-Circle-of-Friends-471.pdf

[74] Reynolds, David. Mightier Than the Sword. New York: Norton. 2011. Print Page XII

[75] Ibid., XIII

[76] Ibid.

[77] Reynolds, David. Mightier Than the Sword. New York: Norton. 2011. Print Page 124-125

[78] Ibid, 162

[79] https://education.nationalgeographic.org/resource/underground-railroad

[80] Clifford-Larson, Kate. Bound for the Promised Land. New York: Ballantine. 2003. Print. Page 46-47

[81] Dilbeck, D.H. Frederick Douglass-America's Prophet. Chapel Hill. 2018. Print. Page 10

[82] Ibid., 14

[83] Ibid., 18

[84] Ibid.

[85] Dilbeck, D.H. Frederick Douglass- America's Prophet. Chapel Hill. 2018. Print. Phillip S. Foner and Yuval Taylor, eds., Frederick Douglass: Selected speeches and writings (Chicago: Lawrence Hill, 1999) Pages 32-37

[86] Ibid.

[87] Ibid.

[88] https://encyclopedia.ushmm.org/content/en/article/aryan-1

[89] (Harvey, 2000, pg. 110.)

[90] Harvey, Paul. Freedom's Coming. North Carolina: North Carolina Press, 2005. Print.

[91] Ibid.

[92] https://kinginstitute.stanford.edu/encyclopedia/southern-christian-leadership-conference-sclc

[93] https://kinginstitute.stanford.edu/king-papers/documents/address-delivered-albany-movement-mass-meeting-shiloh-baptist-church

[94] The Framing of a Right to Choose: Roe v Wade and the Changing Debate on abortion Law," Law and History Review 27 (2009): 281-330

[95] https://humanlifereview.com/the-long-road-of-eugenics-from-rockefeller-to-roe-v-wade/

[96] https://humanlifereview.com/how-paul-weyrich-shaped-the-gop-agenda-part-ii/

[97] https://humanlifereview.com/criss-cross-democrats-republicans-and-abortion-2/

[98] http://www.priestsforlife.org/library/4377-caesar-must-obey-god.

www.ingramcontent.com/pod-product-compliance
Lightning Source LLC
LaVergne TN
LVHW022321080426
835508LV00041B/1651